Trash of the Titans

Mr. Satanism

Published by Inept Concepts, 2013.

While every precaution has been taken in the preparation of this book, the publisher assumes no responsibility for errors or omissions, or for damages resulting from the use of the information contained herein.

TRASH OF THE TITANS

First edition. January 14, 2013.

Copyright © 2013 Mr. Satanism.

ISBN: 979-8227079367

Written by Mr. Satanism.

Introduction

Before the *Lord of the Rings* flicks came out and reminded us why reading is so boring whilst simultaneously breaking box office records (because almost everyone fell asleep halfway through and had to pay to see them twice), most people considered movies about dragons, knights, and wizards to be the stuff of nerds, tolerated by the rest of society only because they inspired the occasional hottie to show up at Comic-Con dressed as Red Sonja. In truth though, Hollywood has a long history of producing classic, high-quality fantasy adventure films, including (and probably limited to) *Jason and the Argonauts, The Seventh Voyage of Sinbad, The Golden Voyage of Sinbad, Sinbad Goes to Camp,* and the criminally-underrated *Dragonslayer,* a movie with a pair so big that they actually let the dragon ruthlessly slaughter the beautiful princess, after which she's gorily devoured by baby dragons (spoiler warning). This book isn't about those movies though. This book is about the movies where the most astounding special effect is a midget, the movies where the actor playing the barbarian weeps bitterly for his career while swatting at a giant snake with a floppy plastic sword, and the movies where the sole saving grace is inarguably the tits. And sometimes even those are sub-par. So put away your weird-looking dice (you fucking geeks), take a break from jerking off to the mom from the *Herculoids,* and steel yourself for a journey into that most fantastical land of shitty moviemaking, courtesy some of the most embarrassing mythological miscarriages to ever drop into the can: the *Trash of the Titans*.

Some Abbreviations You May Need to Know

- D&D – Dungeons & Dragons
- AD&D – Advanced Dungeons & Dragons
- D&D 3E – Dungeons & Dragons, Third Edition
- D&D B&E – Dungeons & Dragons-Related Breaking and Entering
- D&D CSI – Crime Scene Investigation, Nerd Victims Unit
- DM – Dungeon Master
- GM – Game Master
- PM – Pussy Master
- LARP – Live-Action Role-Playing
- NCSGRP – Naughty Catholic Schoolgirl Role-Playing
- d20 – A twenty-sided die
- d8 – An eight-side die
- d2 – A two-sided die
- Tina-Jane Pinkowski – A two-faced bitch, who I'm pretty sure gave me the clap
- (212) 664-7665 – Her phone number

Aladdin

(1992)

Written by Paul Levinson and Nathalie Harrison

I reviewed Disney's 1992 animated classic *Aladdin* on my original *Video Picks* website (now defunct), and again on my subsequent blog *The Mr. Satanism Fix*, and my complaints there aside it really is a great cartoon, a modern monument to magic, wonder, romance, and saturation marketing. This version, from a company called Bevanfield (me neither), not so much. Seriously, why is Aladdin Chinese here? The only explanation I can come up with is that it's some sort of copyright dodge:

BEVANFIELD: No, see, it takes place in *China*. It's not an infringement at all.

DISNEY: Hmm, they win this round. Looks like it's time to have every applicable law radically changed, easily accomplished since we're more powerful than the government.

And that was probably a smart move on Bevanfield's part, since the beginning of this movie is almost exactly the same as the Disney version: (Chinese) Aladdin, accused of stealing fruit, is being chased by guards and vendors all over town, including a detour through the middle of a harem. Here's where things take a turn for the insane though: the fleeing Aladdin bumps into this A-rab, who subsequently summons a genie that looks like what someone who's never seen a black guy before probably imagines one would have looked like in the 1990's, and, to be fair, this hypothetical someone wouldn't have been far off. Seriously, imagine if MC Hammer, stand-up "comedian" Sinbad, Kazaam, and any random NBA player (except the white one) had a four-way love child and he would a) probably look a lot like this genie and b) undoubtedly be hunted down and killed immediately. The genie rescues Aladdin by kicking everyone's ass with kung fu, after which the Arab enlists Aladdin's assistance in obtaining the famous lamp, which just happens to be hidden in a cave in Aladdin's back yard. A cave which opens when the Arab chants the following spell:

"Camel dung,

Little boy's tongue,

Give only the best to me.

Dragon sand,

Elastic band,

Open sesame."

Jesus Christ, that's fucking insane. And did you pick up on the pedophilia subtext? Because I totally picked up on that. Once inside the cave Aladdin is attacked by spiders and snakes, but the genie shows up and saves him again, this time by using his trusty blow torch. When they finally locate the lamp *another* genie appears and informs them that they've been specifically chosen to protect the kingdom and ensure that good conquers evil, so, ignoring this completely, Aladdin uses the magic of his two genies to learn karate (I'm dead serious) and win the hand of the local princess. And by "hand" I mean "pussy", obviously. In the end the Arab steals the lamp and uses it to kidnap the princess and teleport Aladdin's entire palace to his mountain hideout, so Aladdin, the black genie, and a (literal) bald eagle mount a rescue and use karate to defeat the evil Arab's minions, which appear to be the reanimated skeletons of midgets. Or possibly the reanimated skeletons of all those little boys whose tongues gave the best to him. The songs sound like the kind you're allowed to use royalty-free for the price of the CD, Aladdin's mom is named "Madam Dim Sum", there's a part where a dog pisses on the bad guy, and naturally the black genie can't swim.

Ridiculous, racist, and deranged beyond words. It's definitely worth checking out.

Aladdin and the Death Lamp

(2012)

Directed by Mario Azzopardi

Ah, Aladdin and the *Thousand Nights and a Night*. Hidden oases, treasure-laden caravans, Middle Eastern magic, all playing out against the backdrop of majestic, sweeping desertscapes. Leave it to Syfy (AKA the Syphilis Channel) to set their version almost entirely in the woods.

So, some time back these three cats stuffed an evil genie into a lamp and then tossed said lamp into that old quarry just outside of town. You know, they one they flooded for a while and people kept getting busted for swimming there? That's the place. Years later Aladdin, who's graduated from street rat to grave robber, finds the lamp and accidentally frees the genie, after which it goes on a murderous, soul-eating rampage, alternately killing people and letting them punk themselves with poorly-phrased wishes, as dictated by whatever currently serves the lazy, inconsistent script. Adding to Aladdin's problems, his best friend repeatedly betrays him, often to no logical end whatsoever. Seriously, why do people in the movies always feel that they're obligated to keep promises they've made, under duress, to the bad guys? The genie looks like the version of Gollum from that old, 1970's *Hobbit* cartoon, the bad guys use spider-tracers to home in on the good guys, the only non-genie monster of note is a shitty-looking two-headed snake, and there aren't any tits. Oh, and you gotta love how they use the original Arab word for genie, *djinni*, but then have everyone pronounce it "djinn", which is the plural form and thus completely wrong anyway. Not all languages work exactly like English, you know, you WASPy fucks. Try leaving L.A. once in a while so you can learn how the rest of the world works.

Ali Baba and the Seven Saracens

(1964)

Directed by Emimmo Salvi

Ali Baba? The forty thieves guy? At what point in time was he such a draw at the box office that it made any sense whatsoever to just drop him into a random, generic adventure movie? Indiana Jones? Sure. Sinbad the Sailor? Absolutely. The Rock? Up until that stupid fucking tooth fairy movie, why not? But Ali Baba? That's like making an action movie starring Little Red Riding Hood where she isn't re-imagined as a nineteen-year-old ninja who repeatedly shows us her tits. Seriously, besides the whole "open sesame" gimmick, what possible "Ali Baba" lynchpin is there to wrap an entire movie around? Hell, even the *King of Queens* guy has that "dude they go to when John Belushi's brother isn't available" angle to exploit.

Whatever the logic, in this flick Ali Baba leads a group of A-rab insurgents who aren't happy with the cats running their country. Or, in American terms, he's a terrorist. He's almost captured early on after one of his people sells him out under torture (wow the parallels just won't quit, will they?), but he manages to dodge that bullet when this smokin' hot brunette with gigantic tits lends an assist. As it turns out the brunette is somebody important and it's definitely in her best interests to keep Ali Baba at tit's length, but once he manhandles her she's instantly in love so when the authorities catch him five minutes later she won't leave his side and they arrest her too. Eventually they escape with the help of a midget and a eunuch with Tourette's syndrome, during an organized breakout that supposedly goes down at midnight despite the fact that the mid-afternoon desert sunlight is so fucking bright that I'm surprised everyone in the scene didn't immediately burst into flames. Now, I've seen enough bad movies to not be surprised when moviemakers don't know the difference between day and night (Hollywood can be kind of stupid sometimes. Offered as proof: *The Mummy Returns*.), but what really confused me about the jailbreak scene is the role the midget played, and whose interests he was actually serving. I mean, he masterminds the entire escape, but then, inexplicably, asks to be left behind. Ali Baba heroically complies, the midget cries, and then everyone gets caught anyway. It all plays out like your classic set-up ("I'm sorry sir, but Ali Baba was shot trying to escape!"), but later the midget is clearly identified as a good guy so I don't know what the fuck we're supposed to take from all this. I'm tempted to accuse the little bastard of playing both sides against the middle, but I've never been entirely sure what that means, exactly. Nevertheless, I've got my eye on him.

So where were we? Oh yeah, the escape attempt. I said they all got caught, but that's not entirely accurate because Ali Baba and his girl at least do manage to slip away under the cover of, er, broad daylight. But then Ali insists on dicking around and they're captured again, rendering everything that's happened over the last several minutes completely moot. Honestly, movie, if you just wanted to kill some time, why didn't you stick a sex scene in there or something? This time the bad guy decides to decapitate Ali Baba immediately, but Ali is spared when someone suddenly shines a spotlight in his face, because this means that he's the chosen one. (Seriously, I swear that's what happens) Chosen to do what? Fight in some tournament against seven Saracens to see who gets to be the next king. (Note: "Saracen" is Arabic for "towelhead".) If you're guessing that Ali Baba faces off against the main bad guy in the final round of this tournament, wins, and then fucks his hot, big-titted girl up the ass (off-camera) then the joke's on you, because Ali is actually shot in the shoulder by agents of treachery right in the middle of his climactic fight and they wrap it all up with a rebellious uprising instead. (Incidentally, there's a simultaneous harem uprising as well, which, if nothing else, is at least somewhat hotter.) It all sounds action-packed enough, but frankly the whole thing is pretty boring, and the lack of any monsters, over-the-top gore, or tits really put me off my hummus. If there is a potential blockbuster of an Ali Baba movie out there, this definitely ain't it.

Almighty Thor

(2011)

Directed by Christopher Ray

Odin's urinal tract, they shat this thing out so fast – so as to cash in on the (undoubtedly equally dumb) Marvel Comics Thor movie that came out about the same time – that apparently there wasn't even time to shoot any retakes: "A god of the Aesir never give up!" some guy says at one point. Uh, that's never *gives* up, cretin. I guess there was no time to fix shit in post, either.

So, it seems that Booker (*21 Jump Street*) is jonesing to possess the Hammer of the Gods, so he raises one hell of a ruckus, attacking all the other gods with a magical bone (heh) and some giant cartoon hyenas. Odin, pimp of the gods, manages to hide the Hammer before Booker croaks him though, so now Odin's beach bum son Thor and his ugly female associate (seriously, I think maybe she's supposed to be the goddess of ugly) have to go on a quest to find it. Initially this quest entails wandering around in the woods behind Target, but after a while everyone shuffles off to L.A., where Thor and Booker get into a fight in the parking lot. Wow, just like my cousins last weekend. From this point on, it's just a lot of boring back & forth: Thor kills Booker, Booker gets better, Thor shoots Booker with an Uzi, Booker shoots Thor with the Uzi, the ugly chick stabs Booker through the face with a sword (this, incidentally is accomplished via the worst cartoon effect I've seen in months, and seeing as I mainline Syphilis Channel movies, that's saying a lot), Booker sends Thor to Hell, *Thor* gets better... Oh, and somewhere in there the end of the world begins, which sets off every car alarm on the block. Really, there's nothing new here; I'm sure there's a 1990's-era Thor comic book featuring this exact same ~~plot~~ sequence of events, guest-starring Ghost Rider and the Punisher. And even with so much going on this is one of the most uninvolving movies I've ever seen, with an ending so cheap and lazy that it even recycles scenes of destruction from *The 7 Adventures of Sinbad*, another fuck-awful fantasy-hero movie that stinks the place up like the Fenris wolf before he was housebroken. What a waste of time. They should've called this "The Almighty Bore". Wait, that's entirely too obvious, like Leonard Maltin obvious. I'm gonna go with "The Almighty Sack of Piss".

The Archer: Fugitive from the Empire

(1981)

Directed by Nicholas Corea

Okay, I know I did a lot of drugs in the 1980's, but I could have *sworn* that this was a TV series for a while. Can anyone confirm this? I'm not saying it was around as long as *Gunsmoke* or even *Beyond Westworld*, but I clearly remember seeing at least two episodes, unless I actually sat through this one twice, which I can't imagine doing since it's so goddamned boring. It starts with these barbarians deciding to have a treaty, which they just go on and on and on about for nearly half the overall running time. Seriously, it's like watching one of those channels where they make laws or argue public policy, except everyone's dressed like they're at a Renaissance festival, which, now that I think about it, would probably make those public policy channels a lot more entertaining. In fact, if they passed out a few maces and war hammers to use during some of the more heated debates, like whether or not to install a new stoplight in front of the Food Lion, they might even win their time slots occasionally.

Anyway, back to the barbarians. They finally iron out their little peace negotiation and, wouldn't you know it, the Cylons pick that exact moment to launch a sneak attack! Ha ha! Sorry, I couldn't resist. Actually, the barbarians celebrate by getting loaded, and a good time is had by all until these wickedly cool-looking snake men show up, kill the king, and leave his son holding the bag. You know, the bag with all the blame in it. The son heads for the hills with, I dunno, his mentor or teacher or gay lover, whoever this other fucking cat was supposed to be, but said cat soon buys the pasture, forcing the son to recruit some new allies, including one of the hottest goddamned witches I've ever seen, and rest assured, I've associated with some pretty hot witches in my time. Of course the snake men are after our heroes, and later they have to fight a wizard and some zombies too, but I guess they have plenty of hit points because they pretty much dominate. Especially the witch, who, if I haven't mentioned this already, is *one of the hottest goddamned witches I've ever seen*. Seriously, if sacrificing a few blue-eyed Christian babies and kissing the Devil's butthole is all it takes to be on the same team as her, you can sign me the fuck up.

Atlantis: The Lost Continent

(1961)

Directed by George Pal

Dateline - the salad days of ancient Greece. (Yum. Greek salad.) Our main guy and his pop are out fishing when they come across this tasty little number adrift all alone in a boat. They rescue her, but apparently she graduated at the top of ingrate class because she starts bitching almost immediately and doesn't let up until they beat her senseless with an oar and then cut her up for bait. At least that's what I would've done. For some reason they put up with her bad attitude though, right up to the point where she steals off under cover of darkness, and also their boat. The son manages to catch her before she gets too far, but then they make a deal: he'll help her try to find her way home to, get this, *Atlantis,* but if they haven't found "Atlantis" within a month her pussy is his. It's the kind of bet even a Mormon would take – the chick's pretty hot, and the likelihood that Atlantis is actually real is virtually nil – but I still can't believe they just sail off without going back to tell the dad what's going on. Think about it - this poor schmoe is gonna wake up in the morning to find his beloved son *and* his fishing boat, which was his only form of sustenance, inexplicably gone, with no explanation whatsoever. Seriously, what are the odds that he subsequently hung himself? Hovering right around 100%, I'd say.

Junior, as it turns out, doesn't fare much better: not only is Atlantis a real, findable place, it seems that the people who live there are all total dicks. In fact, the only one who isn't a complete bastard is the Chief from *Get Smart!*, but every time he popped up it reminded me of the "Cone of Silence" (the only joke that worthless show seemed to have in its entire arsenal), so before long I ended up resenting him too. Of course the best part of any Atlantis movie is when the place inevitably sinks into the sea, but this time around there's some extra hilarity in the form of the main bad guy, who, while everyone else is running around panicking, just stands there picking people off with a gigantic laser cannon for absolutely no reason other than to be a complete and unapologetic cocksucker. You really have to respect that kind of dedication to evil. It's a weird, ridiculous, inexplicably preachy movie (they even pummel us with some totally out-of-place Christian shit; if I wanted to listen to that I'd actually show up to church *before* the part where they pass out the free wine), but there's plenty of craziness going on and the main chick really is an impressive piece of ass, so overall it's pretty damned entertaining.

Ator, the Fighting Eagle

(1982)

Directed by Joe D'Amato

The Kingdom of the Spider, we are assured, will last for a thousand years and beyond. Just like the Third Reich, and we all know how that turned out. Sure enough, one day this broad pops out a gigantic baby (how she even survived the experience is a mystery to me), who is prophesied to slay the Spider God and then star in many unwarranted sequels. Naturally this doesn't sit well with the leaders of the spider coalition, so they dispatch some soldiers to find the baby. Their only clue to the newborn's location is that he's somewhere on Earth, but, exhibiting an amazing combination of intuition and incompetence, they ride straight to his exact location and kill everyone there *except* the prophecy baby. The baby grows up to be Ator, a buff dork, somewhat brighter than a chimp, with a fairly impressive girlfriend who... *oh my god she's his sister!* Gross. Oh, wait a minute, he *was* spirited off and given to another couple to raise, so obviously she's really his step-sister. Hell, that ain't no big. If my step-sister looked as good as this chick, I would totally hit it. Apparently Ator agrees with me because he marries her, but then the Spider Guild raids his village, kidnaps her, and kills everyone else. Of course he vows revenge, and as he makes his way to the Spider God's lair he engages in various misadventures that are so laughable they'd be parody if this movie was even slightly self-aware. He bones a homely witch. He's confronted by the undead and runs away. He proves incapable of sneaking past several *blind* men, and is forced to slaughter them instead. And he swordfights a *shadow*. That's right, in a special effects first (and last) they had some sorry-ass production assistant holding a sword cast his shadow on the wall, and Ator pretends to fight it. Most people will probably mock the chintzy giant spider Ator faces at the end, but considering his preceeding exploits I was just happy that they didn't wrap things up by pitting him against a basket of kittens, or a guy in a wheelchair wielding a frisbee. All this plus a pretty blonde sidechick, a cute, antic-prone bear cub (likely included to keep the kids and your girlfriend from falling asleep), and a guy who pronounces "herbs", as in the plant, like "Herbs," as in several guys named Herb, which in the context of an preliterate society where he's never seen the word written down, is especially hilarious. Or maybe he's just British. Which is almost as bad.

The Barbarians

(1987)

Directed by Ruggero Deodato

When it comes to circus gypsies vs. rubes, never underestimate the gypsies. After an exciting fight/chase though these gypsies do get caught, and the survivors are enslaved to the man, including two small children who eventually grow up to be meathead goons the Barbarian Brothers. (Remember those guys? That's okay, neither does anyone else.) Naturally they don't like being slaves (except possibly to the rhythm) and they're a constant source of grief to the bad guys, but the main bad guy's hands are tied because he promised not to kill them as part of his bid to get into the gypsy queen's pants. Aye, but there's the rub. No, not in the gypsy queen's pants; I mean the bad guy promised that *he* wouldn't kill them, not that they wouldn't kill each other. After years of torture and Pavlovian conditioning, he pits the brothers against each other in a fight to the death, which I must admit is a brilliantly insidious solution if you've got the patience for it. His plan backfires though, and it's right here that this movie – which has been pretty entertaining up to this point – makes it's first and most fatal mistake: they let the Barbarian Brothers talk. And let me tell you, these two really are a pair of full-blown, neckless retards. (I'm not kidding about their necks - in one part, they can't even be hanged.) Every time they speak – even when it's only one-syllable words – they sound like special ed kids trying to recite the periodic table from memory. Hell, they're so fucking dumb that sometimes they can't even remember how to form words at all, and just stand there making stupid noises. (You probably think I'm kidding. I'm not kidding.) These two dullards are so outshined acting-wise, if not necessarily breast size-wise, by their spunky girl sidekick that it's downright embarrassing. Why didn't they make her the main character, and the Brothers, say, her mute bodyguards or something? Seriously, that would've been a fun movie - the adventures of a cute, scheming little chickie, who, when she gets in too deep, calls in her lunkhead muscle to bust up the place. And why, why, why is there a part where the Brothers kiss? Honestly, aren't the endless shots of oiled-up muscles and shirtless men grappling each other more than enough homoeroticism, even for fans of the Barbarian Brothers?

Beastmaster 2: Through the Portal of Time

(1991)

Directed by Sylvio Tabet

The Beastmaster was an old-school cable television staple; back in the 1980's I must have watched that bitch a hundred times while recovering from hangovers on the couch. And except for the first time, when I misread the *TV Guide* and thought I was watching "The BREASTmaster", I've always enjoyed it. It's just a straight-up fun movie; how can you not dig a barbarian warrior whose primary weapon is ferrets? Making a sequel nine years later was a pretty risky proposition though, because let's face it, the audience just wasn't there. All the kids who liked the original back in 1982 had grown up, and even I had moved on from booze to cocaine, which meant fewer weekday hangovers and more time spent at the office to pay for my habit. And by "at the office", of course, I mean "robbing liquor stores". The first half hour of this followup is okay though, with plenty of fighting plus some clever hints that one of the bad guys has actually visited the future, or Earth, or wherever the hell they are in relation to us. Shit, I was still on board when the cute redhead in the Porsche showed up, because let's face it, there's not much on this or any other world that holds my interest like a cute redhead in a Porsche. Once everyone shuffles off to 1991 Los Angeles though it's all *so* fucking stupid, full of tiresome "moron in a moronic land" bullshit and "hilarious" comedic idiocy, like the part where they drive past a movie theater that's showing... *Beastmaster 2*. Har-de-har, you're so witty and meta, *Beastmaster 2*. Meanwhile the only thing actually moving the story along is a series of oh-so-convenient coincidences, which means that there's no real suspense since the solution to any problem is likely to just fall out of the writer's ass at any given moment. In fact, the only point where there's any suspense at all is when the bad guy is about to step through the portal home, with an armed nuclear device in tow, and the Beastmaster stops him so they can fight. Jesus H. Christ, just let him go, Beastmaster! I don't care if he blows up your planet or not, but you can't let him blow up L.A. That's where Lindsay Lohan lives.

Beyond Sherwood Forest

(2009)

Directed by Peter DeLuise

I'm surprised there aren't more of these Robin Hood/ Dungeons & Dragons mash-ups. I know Robin Hood traditionally fights regular guys, but he does live back in legendary times so why shouldn't he throw down with a few monsters too? It's a fun idea, and if people really go for it maybe they could follow up with more swashbuckler/monster blends, like, say, *Zorro vs. the Chupacabras*.

The story begins just like any other Robin Hood movie, with R. Hood & Associates LLC stealing from the rich and giving to the poor. This sounds pretty altruistic on paper, but remember the old saying: if you give a man a fish, he'll eat for a day, but if you *teach* a man to fish, he'll eat for a lifetime. If I was in Robin Hood's faggy boots, instead of just giving my re-appropriated cash directly to the poor, I'd invest it for them and help their money grow. Plus, if I'm sitting on everyone's share anyway, then I can loan some of it out to folks who need a bigger up-front sum than their allotted portion would otherwise amount to. Of course, I'd have to charge them interest and keep a cut for myself, you know, for my time and trouble. I think 70% sounds fair, seeing as I am doing all the work *and* taking all the risk. Not a bad way to make a living, if I do say so myself. I guess selflessness really is its own reward.

Getting back to the movie, it seems that the sheriff who's always after Robin and his gang is up against the wall this time, so he decides to break out his top-secret weapon - a magical chick who can take two forms: a gigantic dragon, or my fucking **dream girl** because *oh my god she is so fucking hot*. Seriously, if I ever hit that I think I'd find religion, although to be honest it would probably be a religion I made up myself, and that primarily involved worshiping a pair of her soiled panties. Anyway, the dragon's first move is to attack one of the local villages ("You! You're responsible for bringing this plague upon us!" someone says to Robin Hood after this happens. Dude knows this how?), so Robin and his band of merry... Actually, he barely has enough merry men on hand to play bridge much less make up a "band", so we'll just say "and his friends". Robin *and his friends* attack the dragon and chase it away, but not before it kills their fat, Christian buddy. You know, "Tired Fuck" or whatever that guy's name is. Then they all start wringing their hands because the dragon "bled but did not die". Come on, it wasn't hurt all that bad. Is everyone in Robin Hood land a gigantic sissy who faints and bleeds out the instant they get so much as a paper cut? What are they, a bunch of homophiliacs or something? At any rate, in order to learn how to kill the dragon they have to go on a quest (Of course they do. Why don't these people ever have libraries?), which mainly consists of roaming around in a magical wood filled with cartoon animals. (Just like *Winnie-the-Pooh*! Okay, not really.) Of course it all ends with a big donnybrook between Hood & Associates and the bad guys, and I know that when this happens they always have to break out the "hilarious" bit where the little kid bites someone, but through chain mail? Did he really think that was going to work? Really?

Bonus Question: Why do so many movie dragons have all these ratty-looking holes in their wings? Moths?

Black Moon

(1975)

Directed by Louis Malle

This begins with a badger sniffing around in the road for a while, until a car suddenly comes along and blasts it. That's a pretty good way to start a movie, and it's a good thing this does have a decent opener because the rest of it is fucking annoying and doesn't make any goddamned sense whatsoever. The plot, if you can call it that, centers around this cute chick and the endless amount of grief she gets from everyone who crosses her path: the military shoots at her, two people lock her in a room with an irritating old lady who messes with her head and then laughs at her, some naked children beat her up (it generally takes a fair number of children to beat up a fully-functional adult, but they've definitely got the manpower: there are so many naked children running around in this movie that I'd swear it was shot at the trailer park where my mom lives), and even a unicorn turns up and gives her shit. The only thing that kept me watching was the fact that our heroine got progressively more disheveled and bedraggled as her ridiculous ordeals continued, and I was banking on the possibility that sooner or later she'd lose her shirt entirely and we'd get to see her perky little tits. Happily, this is exactly what happens (and they're *nice*), but then she lets the ol' lady suck on 'em, which was really fucking disturbing. Thanks for ruining the only good part of the movie, you pervy fucks. It's all completely random and pointless, and I'd bet the smaller of my nuts (or, in medical terminology, the lesser teste) that this is one of those times were some idiot had an especially fucked-up dream and was so self-important that when he woke up he decided he just had to make a movie out of it, like anyone else would give a damn about his moron hang-ups or the fact that he likes seeing children naked and watching old ladies suck on tits. What kind of weirdo includes both of those things in the same movie anyway? Honestly, you'd think that the pedophilia and the gerontophilia would cancel each other out, but I guess not.

The Blade Master

(1984)

Directed by Joe D'Amato

After some caveman-on-caveman violence that has no relation to the main plot whatsoever, we catch up with widower Ator, the "Fighting Eagle", currently shacked up in a cave with his, ahem, male companion Thong, where he spends his days training, pumping ~~iron~~ rocks, and writing in his journal. ("Dear diary, shirts still haven't come back from the cleaners...") Meanwhile, the local (and, I suspect, only) Bronze Age scientist has been taken hostage by a cat who looks like Genghis Khan by way of a 1970's porno. Why? Because apparently said scientist has skipped a few thousand years of plausible technological progress and invented the goddamned neutron bomb. (You know, the bad guys in *Beastmaster 2* were trying to get their hands on a neutron bomb too. What are the odds that they were surreptitiously ripping off *The Blade Master*?) The scientist's extra-sexy daughter manages to escape though, and per his instructions she makes a beeline for Ator's cave at "the ends of the earth" (don't worry, apparently this is within walking distance) and recruits him to lend a hand. *En route* Ator fights invisible warriors (how budget-conscious of them), frightens off some cavemen with bright lights and loud noises, takes out a kabuki actor and his entire entourage (minus two guys who run away - they were probably agents), fights a giant snake, and ultimately overwhelms the destination bad guys by swooping in on a *modern-day hang glider* and pelting them with explosives. I think it's safe to say that none of us saw *that* coming. It's a ridiculous movie, but I'll have to admit that it isn't boring, and the daughter is so damn fine that her legs alone are almost worth the price of suffering through the rest of it. I wouldn't opt of your welfare benefits just yet, makers of the Ator series, but I suppose you win this round. Bastards.

The Brotherhood III: Young Demons

(2002)

Directed by David DeCoteau

Part 2 in this series was an exploitive piece of trash dedicated almost entirely to showcasing half-naked young men and, truth be told, I was highly offended. Plus it didn't have any good stuff in it, like gore or tits. Well, Part 3 here isn't anywhere near as bad as its predecessor, but it's still pretty worthless. The premise is basically the same, tired scenario that once led to the arrest of several of my high school friends for trespassing: kids breaking into their school at night to play a live-action, non-copyright-infringing variant of Dungeons & Dragons. Now, we all know that this is never a good idea, because when you play Dungeons & Dragons for "real" something *always* goes wrong, whether it's one of the players going so crazy that he eventually takes the lead role in *The Money Pit*, a killer monkey crashing the session and attacking everyone, or just that subtle, creeping realization that if you keep this shit up you'll be at least thirty before you finally get laid. Welp, this time is no exception: before long one of the gamers is possessed and starts turning the rest of the players into demons. After forcing each of them to suck him off, of course. (This is kinda hot, in a rapey sort of way, when he does it to the cute chick, somewhat less so when it comes to all the dudes.) Our possessed guy looks like Klytus from the 1980 *Flash Gordon* (another movie full of fags), nobody actually dies, and naturally the pillow-biter who makes these *Brotherhood* movies couldn't resist including a part where one dude takes a shower in his tighty-whities. It's a failure on every conceivable, non-gay level, and, frankly, most gay levels as well. I mean really, tighty-whities? Jesus.

The Brothers Grimm

(2005)

Directed by Terry Gilliam

Fake heroes meet actual bad guys, learn to be real heroes. Wow, I haven't seen this plot since breakfast. In fact, it's generally why I *skip* breakfast. And did they *really* include the bit where someone goes to see a guy about a thing, but then said guy turns out to be a woman and everyone is utterly astounded? Seriously, what program was this fucking script written on? Final Hack™? I've seen directions on a shampoo bottle show more creativity. You know what I would love to see in a movie? A scene where someone tells the main guy to go to the convent and talk to Sister Rebecca Munchmore, and when he gets there he does thirty spit-takes in a row because *Sister Rebecca Munchmore is a woman!* I mean why not, right? Seriously, if Hollywood still expects us to find it shocking whenever someone who's been sold to us as especially competent turns out to a woman, why not take this to its logical extreme and have the main guy (or guys) assume that *no one* is a woman? Or they could, you know, not be so goddamned sexist, but we all know *that's* never going to happen.

Sexism aside, the rest of this flick is just an endless brown stream of dumb, lazy jokes, surprisingly bad cartoon effects, and cheap potshots at the French. (Fine, so they did get one thing right.) Honestly, so many words and phrases leap to mind when I see hopelessly lazy, connect-the-numbers crap like this: "half-baked", "inept", "tripe", "mail bomb"... It's especially annoying because there is some good shit here if you're patient enough to look for it: the magical forest looks cool as fuck, the twins one of the main guys beds early on are weirdly hot, and there's a great scene where a little kid is eaten by a horse. (If you'd like to prevent a similar tragedy, might I suggest ElectoBraid brand electric horse fencing? Perfect for your stable, riding track, or that secret pasture behind the dog food plant.) None of it even tries to make sense though, and there's nothing here you haven't seen before in movies like *¡Three Amigos!* (1986), *Tropic Thunder* (2008), or *Bruce Campbell vs. His Own Completely Out-of-Control Ego* (2007). They should have called it "The Brothers Lame".

Conan the Barbarian

(1982)

Directed by John Milius

It's really hard to take the 1982 *Conan the Barbarian* seriously anymore, because we all know that Conan is Arnold Schwarzenegger, and Arnold Schwarzenegger is fucking goofy. "Stick around." "It's not a tumor!" "I call them girly men." Back when this flick first came out Arnold wasn't the joke he is today and this wasn't really an issue, but post-*Twins*? Forget it. And what is with the main bad guy? He's played by that fat black dude who did Darth Vader's voice, and, yes, he does *sound* relatively badass, but he *looks* way too soft to be kicking ass and taking names, or even just taking names, in Conan times. Seriously, he reminds me of the fat guy in accounting who comes to the office Halloween party dressed as a viking and just stands there eating cheese dip for the entire evening, so for the next year everyone calls him "The Cheese Dip Viking". Even *Jingle All the Way* Schwarzenegger could take this clown out.

This movie isn't a total wash though. I like the part where the Asian cat who's training Conan kicks another guy in the balls for absolutely no reason, Conan punches out a camel, Conan's entourage fights cartoon ghosts, and towards the end Conan and company crash an orgy and completely demolish the place. Plus there's a crazy witch (how I love them; any crazy witches wanna get a drink this weekend?), an awesome giant snake, the amazing color-changing flowers, tits ranging from superior to mediocre, and of course plenty of gory violence. It does drag in places, but that's okay because this gives you plenty of time to grab another beer from the fridge before the next person gets decapitated. Oh, and a special shout-out to the princess they rescue-kidnap towards the end. What's better than "super hot"? Mega hot? Ultra hot? Jumbo hot? She's all that and more.

Conan the Destroyer

(1984)

Directed by Richard Fleischer

I know I'm in the minority here, but I actually like this sequel a little better than Part 1. Maybe because everything about it feels more like a 1970's Sinbad movie, right down to the music and the fact that it isn't anywhere near gory enough. Except of course the Sinbad movies weren't quite so niggardly with the monsters. For real, there's only three! And frankly two of them are pretty lame. The cartoon dragon does almost nothing, and the mirror monster's big scene – a pro wrestling-flavored bout with Conan – is beyond laughable. And okay, there's too many dumb jokes too - having Conan recognize the exact same camel from Part 1 and deck it again is a stupid fucking bit that would've gotten the writers flogged if I'd been in charge. The painful sub-gag about "my cousin's sister's brother" is even more insulting though. Your cousin's sister's brother would also be your cousin, asshole, why are you jumping through flaming hoops to make it sound so complicated? Seriously, if you're gonna include a "joke" like this in your movie at least have it make some fucking sense, like have the guy say "my cousin's friend's sister" or something. Don't treat us like we're retards. Another problem with this flick is the fact that Grace Jones is in it (cue gender confusion/puking), and Grace Jones is never a welcome addition to anything. Also, why does every evil sorcerer's fortress collapse the moment you defeat him? Who builds these things? "All an illusion," says the token good wizard after the good guys barely escape being crushed by the collapsing walls and shit. Illusion? I think you're a little unclear on the concept, idiot. Still, with everything they got wrong they do manage to trot out a really cool-ass monster at the end, there is some violence, and the little blonde princess at the center of it all is hot as fuck. I've seen plenty of movies with a hell of a lot less to offer.

Conan the Barbarian

(2011)

Directed by Marcus Nispel

Another Conan movie? Who requested that? I'm sorry, but as a general rule these Conan flicks bore the piss out of me. They never have enough mythological creatures in them, despite the fact that they all clearly go down in some vague, Dungeons & Dragons-style time period. Shirtless guys sword fighting is all well and good if you're into that sort of thing (hey, you need something to watch while you're oiling up your muscles and listening to your Erasure), but for my money a flick like this needs monsters too, and lots of them. This does feature all the blood and violence and tiresome badassery you'd expect from a Conan movie, but truth be told it all wears a little thin after a while, and some parts of the climactic fight scene are just too much to swallow, like when they're stuck down a well or something on this big round thing that keeps... I dunno, slipping, I guess, and flipping over and over like a coin, sort of. See, it's so ridiculously complicated that I can't even describe it, much less buy that it's happening to someone. In the end, the best thing about this movie is the bad guy's cruel, bloodthirsty, goth, incest-*would*-be-best-if-I-could-just-talk-my-dad-into-it daughter (*so* my type). She was yummy-fine, and I was pretty irritated when Conan cut her hand off, pushed her over a ledge, and she fell to her death. I'll tell ya, I would've paid good, cash money to get to *that* body while it was still warm.

Darkest Knight III: The Ultimate Sword

(2003)

Directed by Harley Cokeliss and Mark Ezra

Hey, it's *Darkest Knight III*, the sword & sorcery flick so highly regarded that it's not even listed on the Internet Movie Database, and even the movie my editor wrote is on there. *[Fuck you, Nigel. -Ed.]* We open with a daring raid on the bad guy's mint, and said bad guy's subsequent hissy-snit. His blatantly-treacherous court magician (Fantasy Stock Character #8) has a plan to deal with the thieves though: he's gonna track down this magical sword that has "absolute power over life and death", which I assume means that you can use it to kill people. You know, just like any other sword. Not exactly the most vexing of evil schemes, but nevertheless the good guys decide that he must be stopped, or at least the main good guy decides this. The others are far too busy dealing with some sideplot about getting their king out of hock, which I can only assume is leftover bullshit from *Darkest Knight II: Also Not Listed on the Internet Movie Database*. There's a comedic relief thief (Fantasy Stock Character #5); a mediocre redhead (which, as we all know, is the equivalent of a considerably hotter chick who isn't a redhead); a giant Venus flytrap that looks more like a humongous, diseased vagina (don't ask - I just know); magical eggs that explode like grenades; a sword in a stone except the stone is actually a table; time travel; a skeleton biting someone on the ass; sitcom-level antics involving a love potion; and more. All of which, ironically, adds up to less. Truth be told it's like something a third grader would write, except with less energy. I mean, there's *actually* a scene in this movie where two people rush the main guy from opposite directions, he steps out of the way, and they accidentally stab each other. My favorite though has to be the long shot of the old wizard's cave, which we see at least twice. Are those electrical transmission towers in the background? I think they are. Oh, *Darkest Knight III*, in the end it really is your professionalism that I respect.

Darkon

(2005)

Directed by Luke Meyer and Andrew Neel

It is a time of unrest in the realm of Darkon...

I'll bet it is, you fucking dorks. This documentary is about a bunch of idiots who run around in parks, behind schools, and occasionally at Denny's pretending Dungeons & Dragons is real and hitting each other with sticks. Ah ha ha ha ha ha ha! It's every fantasy-nerd cliché you ever imagined but assumed couldn't really be true, fully confirmed and unreeling right before your eyes. One geek in this movie *actually says* "I'm 28, I live in my parents' basement..." My favorite though is the fat guy who's a loser in real life *and* a pariah in the make-believe world of "Darkon". How fucking pathetic is that? What is he supposed to do now? Create a make-believe world *inside* the make-believe world? I definitely see a shooting spree in his future. Christ, what a bunch of goons. You know what would be awesome? Finding out where they're gonna play next, barging in there dressed like robots, blasting everyone with Super Soakers, and then telling them that they're *all* dead because you're from the future and were sent back in time to wipe out virgins. Then you could add insult to injury by defiling some of their hot elf women, assuming any of them actually *are* hot of course. Which, if this flick is any indication, is pretty unlikely.

Deathstalker and the Warriors from Hell

(1988)

Directed by Alfonso Corona

Deathstalker 1 is stacked to the rafters with so many tits and so much rape that the first time I saw it I was half-convinced that I'd died and accidentally been re-routed to the Heaven for virgin Dungeon Masters who have been charged with aggravated stalking. (I know that sounds pretty niche, but trust me, it exists. God has all the bases covered.) *Deathstalker 2* is even better: not only is it fall-down, piss-yourself hilarious (on purpose), but it also happens to star Monique Gabrielle – one of the hottest, coolest chicks of all time – and not only do we get to see her rack, we get to see a *great deal* of her rack. That's a lot to live up to, and *Deathstalker 3* here fails in every way imaginable and a few no one's even thought of yet. We open at an especially chintzy Renaissance festival, except it turns out that it's really supposed to be the Renaissance. Presently this rampaging hoard of chowderheads shows up to ransack the place, so Deathstalker, who happens to be hanging around, stabs a few of them and then escapes with the hottest piece of ass on hand, who, unfortunately, ends up getting killed before he has a chance to fuck and/or rape her. Later he teams up with the dead chick's twin sister (how convenient, especially for the casting director) to defeat a bald dork and his pathetic zombie slaves, who spend too little time preying on the living and too much time sitting around a campfire, jerking off. (At least that's what I assume they were doing, since one of them clearly has spooge all over his hands.) Seriously, this piss-rotten sequel is an total insult to the Deathstalker name. The only part with any merit whatsoever is when 'Stalker molests the sister, because at least we get to see one of her excellent little tits.

Dragonlance: Dragons of Autumn Twilight

(2008)

Directed by Will Meugniot

I've never read a Dragonlance book and I never will, so if this cartoon is a complete affront to all they stand for don't bother sending me a tear-stained e-mail full of indignation and misspelled words telling me all about it, because frankly I don't give a shit. Which I why I get laid and you don't. The backstory is your usual convoluted twaddle about gods and prophecies and whatnot so I pretty much ignored it, but what I couldn't ignore was the terrible potluck animation that was half old-school and half computer-generated. Seriously, what pinhead thought that this was a good idea? It kind of reminded me of that 1978 *Lord of the Rings* cartoon that was a mix of normal animation and animation drawn over real live people, which looked so goddamned awful that they just stopped halfway through the story and dropped the whole damn thing so as to avoid embarrassing themselves any further. Way to learn nothing from your own niche genre's shitty past, *Dragons of Autumn Twilight*.

Anyway, let's cut to the quest here, which involves a magical staff, some compact discs, and of course several dragons, and is undertaken by a collection of the usual D&D types (knight, dwarf, elf, half-elf, quarter-elf, just-enough-elf to qualify for public assistance, sorcerer, chick, etc.), all of whom are boring, unlikable, or annoying. I especially hated the spasmo, midget elf, who I prayed would come to a particularly painful end, like, say, being eaten alive by one of his natural predators while on fire, bleeding from the anus, and crying pitifully for his mother. (I forget, what is the elf's primary natural predator? It's reindeer, right? I'm pretty sure it's reindeer.) Opposing the heroes are goblins, dragon men, and ghosts, and in their corner are all the gay monsters: unicorns, centaurs, flying horses, and hobbits. They left out the most feared of all gay monsters though, the pink dragon (*draco homo*), whose breath weapon turns you into a queer. (Oh, it's a real D&D monster all right. I'm pretty sure it first appeared in the *Fiend Folio*. I think somewhere towards the back.) There is a smattering of gore, but for the most part this is completely unwatchable, and there's tons of goofy shit that's never adequately explained at all, like why the unicorn looks like she just fought her way out of a vineyard and almost didn't make it. Maybe some of this is explained in the books, but I'll never know because after watching this sun-dried turd I am done with any and all of this Dragonlance crap. I'd rather spend the evening lancing a boil.

Dragon's Blood

(CBS Storybreak)

(1985)

Written by Michael Reaves

CBS Storybreak was a program hosted by Captain Kangaroo that featured a different children's book every week, each re-imagined as a really shitty cartoon. Its primary legacies are being regularly confused with a completely different show called *CBS Schoolbreak Special*, and baffling the fuck out of an entire generation of geeks who, to this day, can't remember whether they really saw an animated version of *Dragon's Blood* as a kid, or just imagined it. Well it's real all right, and while I've never read the book I can tell you that the cartoon goes down on an alien planet, where the green-skinned locals breed dragons for sport fighting. They're like a bunch of extraterrestrial Michael Vicks. One day, this indentured slave named (I swear to God) "Jackin'" decides to steal a baby dragon from his boss and train it on the sly, never mind the fact that a) this is a ridiculously impractical plan and b) another slave named (I further swear to God) "Lickhard" has a grudge against him and certainly wouldn't mind seeing him busted for unauthorized use of stolen dragon. Jackin' pulls it off though (heh), ultimately entering his dragon in a glorified cockfight held in Krakow, former capital of Poland. This is a pretty chintzy production and will probably piss off anyone who likes the book, but now that you know it exists you just have to see it, don't you? Ha ha! Good luck with that. DVD-R burns from my taped-off-TV VHS original start at 600 dollars, unless you're a cute chick with no shame, in which case we can probably work something out.

Dragon's Lair: "Tale of the Enchanted Gift"

(1984)

Directed by Charles A. Nichols

Dragon's Lair was a 1980's video game that was infuriating difficult to play, to the point where the one at the 7-11 near my house was vandalized on a regular basis. (And you can rest assured I told the manager who did this. It was some black kids.) It looked wicked as hell though, like a real cartoon, and the animation was so fucking good that I still have wet dreams about the hot little princess you're meant to rescue at the end. When they announced that there was going to be an honest-to-fuck Saturday morning cartoon based on the game people were ecstatic, but our hopes were cruelly dashed when it turned out to be a dumbed-down piece of garbage that ranked right up there with the video game-inspired cartoons starring Q*Bert and Donkey Kong Jr. Of course the animation is pretty shitty compared to the game, but that would be excusable if anything else about this show was any good. Unfortunately, that's not the case. For example, in the game the main guy, Dirk the Daring, comes across as a slightly goofy everyman who's nevertheless doing his best to save the princess so he can get a taste of that sweet, sweet ass. Believe it or not, he's actually kind of relatable. In the cartoon though, he's portrayed as a raging dork, a medieval nerd who's so easily fooled that he might as well have a sign taped to his back that says "Give me the black plague". Seriously, if I was this guy I'd kick my *own* ass. In this premiere episode he's tricked (via a note slipped under the door) into bringing this golden Maltese Falcon into the castle, where it immediately comes to life and kidnaps the princess. (This is similar to a later episode of *Disney's Adventures of the Gummi Bears*, where a stone gargoyle similarly Trojan horsed into the castle comes to life and tries to murder the king. Disney isn't exactly known for not stealing so I wouldn't be surprised if they ripped this installment of *Dragon's Lair* off wholesale, but to their credit at least the *Gummi Bears* episode is actually good.) At a time when a truly great sword & sorcery cartoon like *Dungeons & Dragons* was airing, this is lazy, collect-my-minimum-wage shitwork, pure and simple. The only good thing about it is the gimmick where they occasionally show us what would have happened if Dirk made different choices, because what generally happens is that Dirk dies. And you know what? I like seeing this incarnation of Dirk the Daring die. Fuck him. And fuck this cartoon.

Dungeons & Dragons

(1983-1985)

Directed by John Gibbs

You might want to sit down and hold onto your dick (if you're a chick, you can hold onto mine), because this is the *greatest Saturday morning cartoon ever made*. It's about these six kids who go on a funhouse ride that obviously needed a safety inspection, because halfway through their car flies off the tracks and carries them to the Realm of Dungeons & Dragons, which if you've ever played the game you know is a land filled with magic, monsters, fabulous treasure, and boring, incomprehensible statistics with names like "THAC0". Of course the kids want to get back home (for all the Realm's benefits, you can't get a decent cup of coffee to save your life), but the only cat willing to help is this hippie dwarf with male-pattern baldness and he's worse than useless, so they end up wandering around fighting crazy monsters and occasionally falling in love just to break up the mind-numbing monotony of fighting crazy monsters all the time. (Trust me, once you've faced off against a flying cyclops head with tentacle eyes, a giant purple worm, and a living bed sheet that performs impromptu plastic surgery on people, nothing makes an impression anymore.) It sounds like your typical kids' adventure show, but the people who made this must have been trying to get fired or something because they included all sorts of questionable shit guaranteed to give parents conniption fits: there's an episode where the kids hook up with a displaced Nazi, there's one where they accidentally summon the Devil and he devastates the entire fucking planet, and there's even one where the good guys decide to openly murder the main villain, a big no-no in 1980s' kids' shows because they were supposed to be all non-violent and shit, which is why nothing ever got accomplished in any of them. (Think about it: how quickly would they have wrapped up the story of the smurfs if Papa Smurf had simply taken a stick and stabbed Gargamel in the eye while he was passed out drunk or something?) Of course they still couldn't show blood spewing everywhere or naked chicks (which is too bad, because cartoon or no, the little redhead in this show, with her super-short miniskirt and thigh high boots, is hot enough to make you go through puberty a second time), but they got away with just about everything else and the end result is like an oil drum full of awesome bouncing right off your skull. You know, in a good way. Seriously, if you don't surf over to Amazon and buy this on DVD right now then there's no other explanation: you're a pussy. It rocks harder than anything that doesn't involve two drunk girls at the same time has ever rocked before.

Dungeons & Dragons: Wrath of the Dragon God

(2005)

Directed by Gerry Lively

I swear, every fantasy movie is exactly the same, the only real defining characteristics being monster density and quantity/quality of tits. There's always this *thing* these people need to *find*, and they always have to go on a long, boring *quest* to get it. It's so fucking gay. Just once I wanna see a fantasy movie where they can have the thingamabob they need delivered, so we can skip all the walking around and get down to business. This time around though our heroes need an orb, and even these days you don't see a lot of stores with a decent orb selection, so I guess ordering it online wouldn't have worked even if they'd thought of it. So what do they need the orb for, you ask? Okay, fine, just pretend you asked, okay? Stop making this difficult. They need the orb because in the wrong hands (i.e. not theirs) it can be used it to awaken this huge dragon that is sure to go completely batshit bonkers and trash pretty much everything. He is so not a morning person. Of course the dude organizing the quest recruits a typical sampling of the usual suspects – a tough chick; a short guy who's supposed to be funny; a fag; and a hot, bitchy elf – and of course they all wander around forever whilst going on and on about stupid shit like the "Goblins of Kirdle" and the "Pool of Sight" and who knows what the fuck until they finally claim the orb, after which the goddamned dragon wakes up anyway. Way to completely waste everyone's time, *Wrath of the Dragon God*. Jesus. Since the hot elf never gets naked, the only part of this movie worth seeing is when the fag is eaten by a (different) dragon that subsequently explodes, leaving undigested pieces of the fag strewn all over the place. If this were an actual game of Dungeons & Dragons, this is the point where the fat loser playing the fag would flip out, accuse the Dungeon Master of cheating, and throw his Mountain Dew at him. Even without that additional level of hilarity though, this scene is still pretty entertaining.

Forbidden Zone

(1980)

Directed by Richard Elfman

This is one of those movies that's weird as fuck just for the sake of being fucking weird, plus it's in black & white, which is the primary indicator that you're dealing with pretentious, art-school bullshit. Black & white is only acceptable if a movie is really old, or if you're trying to trick people into thinking it's really old, like if you're shooting a fraudulent stag film starring Hitler or something. (Hey, you know *Stern* magazine would buy it.) I'm sorry, but if color film is available and you're shooting in black & white anyway, you're a grade-A douche, and I know they had color film in the 1980's, I remember from *Miami Vice*. As for the "plot", in classic art-school fashion it's just a parade of nonsensical horseshit. Short version: this cute French chick (full disclosure: I wouldn't mind fisting her forbidden zone) gets lost in a magical dimension run by Tattoo from *Fantasy Island*, where her retard family eventually arrives to rescue her. The sole reason to watch this is because King Tattoo's daughter, who is smokin', spends the entire running time topless. (Technically, I guess that's *two* reasons to watch it.) Actually, there are a lot of tits in this movie, and the songs, which are by Oingo Boingo, are pretty decent too. I suppose if you're a big fan of Tattoo, tits, and Oingo Boingo, you could do a lot worse. Of course, you could titty-fuck a hottie while watching *Fantasy Island* and listening to *Dead Man's Party* and you'd be doing a helluva lot better.

The Gamers

(2002)

Directed by Matt Vancil

Did I ever tell you about the time I picked up a chick while playing Dungeons & Dragons? And no, she wasn't some fattie wearing elf ears, she was an honest-to-fuck hottie who didn't know a d8 from 8 inches of d. It all started when I wanted to get drunk with some of my married buds. Of course their wives got pissy about this immediately, because a) I like to defy MADD by talking people into driving drunk, and b) the wives knew that I'm a pimp and tons of hot ass would be hanging around. So we compromised. We would get drunk at Eddie's place (he was one of the married guys) while playing Dungeons & Dragons, thus insuring that no one would have to drive, and that any girls who did show up would leave immediately. And this is almost what happened, except one chick did stick around and forced her cute friend to stay too, and even though I'd never met the friend before and she was totally aghast that we were playing D&D, a few drinks later we snuck off together, slipped into Eddie's eight-year-old daughter's bedroom, and did it right there on the floor. So how does this apply to *The Gamers*? It doesn't, it's just an awesome anecdote that proves how goddamned pimp I really am. As for *The Gamers*, well, did you ever hear the Dead Alewives routine about Dungeons &

Dragons? This is basically that, except we jump back and forth between watching the geeks play and seeing their imaginary characters actually act out their ridiculous decisions, leading to humorous juxtapositions. Well, that's the idea anyway, but truth be told the bits they came up with just aren't that funny. The problem is that it's all too goddamned obvious (if you're the right kind of nerd), while being ridiculously obscure at the same time (if you're anyone else). It's like the movie equivalent of a mediocre stand-up act that's performed entirely in Klingon, and at the end of *that* day I'll take banging a complete stranger on a child's bedroom floor any time. Provided we don't actually wake the child up next time, because damn, that was awkward.

The Gamers: Dorkness Rising

(2008)

Directed by Matt Vancil

The bits are somewhat less obvious in this sequel to *The Gamers* (2002), and there's even an actual story this time around: the DM running the game is trying to write his very own official Dungeons & Dragons adventure (dare to dream, idiot), but no one can beat his beta test version until a female newbie joins their campaign and shows all the seasoned nerds how it's done. As a general rule I'm not a big fan of the "chicks can do everything better than guys, even dumb shit they normally have no interest in, because all men are idiots" approach to comedy (if I was, this would be a book about the TV show *Home Improvement*), but it mostly works here, plus the girl in question is just cute enough that I found myself desperately aching to bone her. She's a doggy chew toy compared to the actress who plays the hot blonde sorceress though, but be careful: sometimes the sorceress is played by a dude, and if you're whacking it to her and happen to climax at the wrong moment you might find yourself developing some crippling sexual orientation issues, and then you'll never pick up a hot chick while playing Dungeons & Dragons. Did I ever tell you about the time I did that? For real, that totally happened.

The Greatest American Hero: "Wizards and Warlocks"

(1983)

Directed by Bruce Kessler

Initially, *The Greatest American Hero* was a terrific show with a brilliant gimmick: dude has a suit that gives him superpowers, but he lost the instruction manual so slapstick disasters repeatedly occur. By the time this installment (one of the last) was produced though, the stories had become increasingly retarded, to the point where I'm not exaggerating when I say that this isolated 48 minutes of television might be one of the stupidest fucking things I've ever seen.

The episode begins with some college drips playing a prop-heavy Dungeons & Dragons proxy that also incorporates elements of hide-and-seek and awards players bonus points for playing old Intellivision games at the video arcade. Obviously someone did their research, because that's *exactly* how Dungeons & Dragons works. There's a problem though: it seems that the drip who's, well, hiding, is the unwitting target of a kidnapping plot, so the Greatest American Hero and his friends have to find him before it's – you guessed it – too late.

Complicating this, of course, is the fact that the rules governing "Wizards and Warlocks" consist entirely of smugly-written, incomprehensible gibberish. Seriously, listen to this asinine shit:

SUPER-HOT MAIN CHICK: "Only a rook, huh? Then you are vulnerable to the blade and Sarnak."

BOB SAGAT: "Not unless you've survived the giant leech over the heights of Zervos."

(Yes, this episode really features Bob Sagat, playing a college nerd who is wise in the ways of the Leech of Zervos. And what's really sobering about this is that *Full House* was still four years in his future and *America's Funniest Home Videos* six, so at this point his career hasn't even bottomed out yet.)

Of course our (greatest American) heroes are forced to play Wizards and Warlocks in order to find the missing student, and along the way they meet the guy who invented the game (portrayed, of course, as a cowardly *über* dork), wander around in the steam tunnels underneath the school (an obvious nod to the real-life case where a kid disappeared for weeks after playing Dungeons & Dragons in steam tunnels beneath his own school, never mind that this story turned out to be a full-blown hoax and the kid in question was actually hiding under a friend's bed the entire time), and run their sole gag ("Isn't Dungeons & Dragons weird? It's so weird!") so far into the ground that, this very minute, a family in China isn't laughing at it either.

Online research suggests that ABC canceled *The Greatest American Hero* just before this episode would have aired, and I must say, at this point I fully support their decision. God almighty.

Hägar the Horrible

(1989)

Written by Douglas Wyman

Technically this cartoon does fall within the parameters of this book, but the only reason I'm including it is for the "Holy shit, that exists?" factor. I mean really, who knew that there was a *Hägar the Horrible* cartoon? Even more surprising is the fact that it's actually pretty funny. "The faster we row, the faster we'll be home with our wives and kids," Hägar tells his men, at which point everyone starts rowing in the opposite direction. There's a square globe. A monk runs a business called "Copies While U Wait". And to their credit, they actually let Hägar and his associates be what they're ostensibly supposed to be: violent, illiterate marauders who live in the Dark Ages, something the comic strip tends to downplay what with its aversion to rape jokes and all. They fight, they drink beer, and in one part, when a pissed-off Hägar is literally drowning a guy by forcing an entire barrel of beer down his throat, Lucky Eddie says "Hey! Looks like drinks are on Hägar!" Now that's viking humor. They only made this one episode, but that's okay because, as good as it is, it really is a one-note idea. Not that this has stopped the comic strip from dragging it out for 40+ years now.

Hawk the Slayer

(1980)

Directed by Terry Marcel

Hawk the Slayer (Hank the Slayer to his friends) has some major issues with the spasmo who used to host *Ripley's Believe It or Not*, who killed his girl *and* his dad, and in separate incidents, even. Of course he's contractually obligated to seek revenge, but for some reason he bides his time for *years,* despite the fact that Mr. or Not has spent the interim running completely amok and wrecking all sorts of gratuitous havoc, and despite the additional fact that Hawk has an ace in the hole: a magical sword with a bunch of ill-defined, low-rent powers, the most obvious of which is the hand carved into the hilt that functions like an actual, living hand. If this dude ever drops his keys down a sidewalk grate, he is *set*. Of course, I can think of way better uses for the hand than that. I'd probably never leave the house.

So anyway, somehow the bad guy's latest scheme – kidnapping a nun and demanding an impossible ransom for her return – finally motivates our hero to do something besides ride around on his horse while his idiotic disco theme music plays, so with the help of a blindfolded witch (don't be such a drama queen, toots, everyone else is just as embarrassed as you are) and those spinning hula hoop thingies from *Superman II*, he cobbles together a third-rate fellowship consisting of a giant (a slightly taller than average dude with male pattern baldness), an elf (a nasally fag sporting Mr. Spock ears), and a dwarf, who eats raw fish whole and isn't even played by a real dwarf. (If there's a Dwarf Actor's Guild, they should seriously consider levying a moderate fine.) The fellowship's strategy: steal the ransom from someone else, and then pay it. Wait, what? What kind of a cowardly, cop-out scheme is that? Fortunately, this ridiculously passive-aggressive plan doesn't quite pan out, so they're actually forced to be heroic and as a result there is some fighting at the end, during which the witch breaks out her impressive magical arsenal, which includes a can of Silly String and – I kid you not – Super Balls. And I don't mean that, metaphorically, she has a humongous pair; I'm talking about the actual rubber balls you get out of the gumball machine. There's a scene where dozens of the things come flying right at the bad guys, and given the budget on display here I can't help but picture some hapless PA standing outside the grocery store with a roll of quarters, buying the goddamn things one... at... a... time.

Hell's Labyrinth

(2008)

Directed by Drew Maxwell

Our main chick is creamed with one of those long-bladed shovels (I believe it's called a spade, but I'm not sure if it's politically correct to use that term nowadays; I know you can't call them "Alabama porch-monkey thwackers" anymore), and when she comes to she finds herself in a mysterious labyrinth, alongside several other people, none of whom know what the fuck they're doing there either. The locals are definitely hostile though: in no time flat they're bum-rushed by monsters, and the rest of the movie basically amounts to an AD&D dungeon crawl where the Random Encounters table looks something like this:

1. Spiky cartoon monster
2. Spiky cartoon monsters (2-4)
3. Zombie horde
4. Naked chick

Yeah, I'm definitely not liking those odds. At first I assumed that the entire cast was already dead and unknowingly condemned to Purgatory/Limbo/Hell/Detroit/a J.J. Abrams series, a not-so-surprising revelation most movies still treat like a shocking twist ending despite the fact that it's almost as common as the ending where the hero gets the girl. Thankfully they torpedo this possibility early on, and ultimately it turns out that they're all just trapped in an alternate dimension where they're meant to serve as sacrifices for a bunch of humanity-hating monsters. What a relief, right? It's another one of those horror flicks that's so washed-out it might as well be in black & white (seriously, who decided that color wasn't scary anymore?), and they use more fake computer backgrounds than all three of the Star Wars prequels combined, but the part where the good guys have to maneuver their way through a tunnel filled with barbed wire is effectively gruesome, there is some gore and full-frontal, and the actual twist ending isn't half bad. I wouldn't call it a *good* movie, exactly, but at least there's *some* hustle going on. Just barely worth a look if Netflix isn't streaming the David Bowie/ Muppet *Labyrinth* this month.

Hercules Against the Moon Men

(1965)

Directed by Giacomo Gentilomo

Okay, the first two people Hercules agrees to help out in the course of our story end up impaled to death and shot in the chest with an arrow, respectively. Then, when Hercules tries to rescue a girl who's about to be sacrificed to monsters, the bad guys catch him in a goddamned *net* without even breaking a sweat! Might want to leave this one off your resume, Herc. The bad guys put Hercules in a giant waffle maker, but when he's too tough to perforate the evil queen who's masterminding all these shenanigans decides to make him her love slave instead. Bitch ain't bad, but the brunette Hercules threw in with previously is considerably hotter so Hercules fakes the queen out and when the time is right he tells her to suck rainwater and starts busting the place up. Pretty much everybody on the queen's staff betrays her at this point (should've spread it around a little more, baby), so she goes to her silent partners the space aliens for help. The aliens are tired of her slutty incompetence though, so they squash her. When Hercules shows up several minutes later one of the aliens clocks him upside the head, but naturally this just pisses him off, so he proceeds to knock stuff over until something turns out to be load-bearing and the aliens' entire hideout collapses right on top of them. And that's the end of that. Another challenge well met, Hercules. More or less.

Hercules in the Haunted World

(1961)

Directed by Mario Bava

People are working hard, scoring with hot women, combing their arm hair in the sun... life is good. Not for long though, because several malcontents have just arrived to kidnap some of them. "You know how much gold the king will pay us," the lead malcontent assures his lackeys, even though he refuses to tell them who, exactly, they're there to kidnap. I guess these criminals are working on the honor system, which is pretty ironic when you think about it. The kidnapping ultimately fails to go off when Hercules unexpectedly crashes the party, but the aforementioned king has plenty more tricks up his sleeve: it seems he's already turned Hercules's's's's... er, 's... turned his girl into a spaced-out zombie, and Hercules, being none the wiser (nothing new here) is forced to found Quest for the Cure, a charitable organization that... Oh, wait, sorry, he's forced to *go on* a quest for the cure. Okay, that makes a lot more sense. The quest involves a tour of Hades, with several acts of questionable daring-do along the way, including stealing a guy's boat, climbing a tree during a lightning storm (it's fun kids, try it!), throwing a monster through a wall, resisting diabolical pussy (this one always trips me up), leaping into a sea of flames, and various other instances of fist-pumping horseshit. Hercules gets the job done and makes it back in one piece though, only to be cornholed by the evil king (for power), *and* his best friend (for pussy). Fortunately, it's nothing that beating the absolute shit out of everybody can't fix, so in the end Herc comes out okay. You'd think that with all the insanity on display (and believe me, I left tons of shit out) this would be a pretty entertaining movie, even if only by accident. But nope, it's all boring as hell (heh), and seems to last twice as long. On the plus side, it does end with the comedic relief drowning himself. I wish more movies featuring comedic relief would end that way.

Highlander II (Renegade Version)

(1991)

Directed by Russell Mulcahy

Everyone knows that *Highlander II* is an unbelievable pile of ass-sucking shit; you could write an encyclopedia about all the things in this movie that don't make any sense whatsoever or are just completely retarded. I mean, we've got the Highlanders suddenly turning out to be aliens, dead guys popping back to life for no reason, a subway train that can go 673 miles an hour, the main dude being attacked by chicken men... It's a fucking joke. Well, apparently this is the "Renegade Director's Cut" or something, where they supposedly went back and fixed everything that sucked. Don't be fooled though - all they did was make the damn thing 20 minutes longer! Fucking *assholes*. If you were being raped in prison, would you want it to last 20 minutes longer? To be fair, they did change one thing: instead of the Highlanders being aliens, now they're *time travelers*. Yeah, that's less moronic. The fact that they released it *twice* proves that this isn't just a movie made by people who are lousy at making movies - this is a movie made by people who *actively hate your fucking guts*. The only good thing about it is the main chick, who is a pretty choice piece of ass. The Highlander screws her in this version (though not as hard as the movie's screwing us, of course), but we never actually see her naked which means the audience still gets zilch out of the deal. Then again, she probably didn't get much out of it either, what with his "problem" and everything. That is what they mean by "the quickening", right?

Highlander: The Final Dimension

(1995)

Directed by Andrew Morahan

They made *Highlander 2* as different from *Highlander 1* as they possibly could without adding a talking dog, and it sucked epic amounts of shit. So they made *Highlander 3* (that's this one) as *similar* to *Highlander 1* as they could and guess what? It still eats piss. There's a crazy dude who thinks he's Napoleon (this bit wasn't even original while Napoleon was still alive), a bad guy who eats a condom, a hilariously fake Photoshop job of the main Highlander in some old photograph, hours of the main Highlander posing with his sword (it's like watching a gay Dungeon Master's wet dream), and of course a big fight that goes down in one of those factories that, from all appearances, manufactures fire by shining blindingly bright lights through gigantic fans. Leave it to the fucking Highlander series to just get around to using overdone late-1980's shit like the fire/fan factory in 1995. And what the hell is this "final dimension" they're blathering about? I was hoping it meant that this would actually be the final Highlander movie, but like Jason and Freddy before him the christfucking Highlander has a pretty malleable definition of the word "final", which, needless to say, promises many more years of misery to come. Fuck you, Highlander.

Highlander: The Source

(2007)

Directed by Brett Leonard

Highlander is the source all right, the source of all my misery. Seriously, how many of these stupid-ass movies are they gonna make??? It's like having chronic diarrhea - more and more shit just keeps coming out. This one's pretty hell-bent on not making any sense whatsoever (and if you don't like it, you can go fuck yourself), but I *think* it's about a quest by several Highlanders to discover the source of their powers. I thought they already explained this: the Highlanders have powers because they come from outer space, until they changed it and decided that they were actually time travelers. So now they're changing it again? Dammit, all these explanations are ridiculous anyway so just pick one and stick with it, you addle-brained fucks. Pretty much everything about this movie blows, but the absolute worst has to be the bad guy: he looks like a gay albino biker, emotes like a pro wrestler (except without all the subtlety and nuances), runs around all sped up like he's chasing Benny Hill, and of course when he first appears he's dressed like a rooster. What is it with these movies and bad guys who look like chickens? And why does the (not so) thrilling climax go down at Burning Man? This sequel actually premiered on the Sci-Fi Channel, and that's generally where shitty ideas go to die, so hopefully this'll be the last we hear of these alien time-traveling rooster pricks for a while. Suck my balls, Highlanders. Suck. My. Fucking. Balls.

Highlander: The Search for Vengeance

(2007)

Directed by Yoshiaki Kawajiri

For God's sake, how much more of this pinhead crap are we expected to put up with? In *Highlander 1* the main guy killed every other Highlander around, which as I understand the premise should pretty much exhaust every possible story you could tell about this clown, unless he subsequently decided to coach an underdog Little League baseball team made up of lovable misfits or something. But somehow they've managed to churn out six more movies, two TV series, and a cartoon, plus innumerable comic books, novels, video games, music videos, book & record sets, radio shows, penny dreadfuls, gravestone rubbings, cave paintings, and now here's a goddamned japanimated version that's got him running around in the future fighting mutants and robot spiders. For real, I am so sick of the christing Highlander. Still, props where they're etc.: at least the japanimated Highlander is a much bigger badass than the movie and TV incarnations. (Are all these Highlanders even supposed to be the same guy? Actually, never mind - I don't want to meet the person who knows enough about Highlander to answer that question.) There's plenty of blood, some tits, and the giant crocodile that shows up in one part is pretty damn cool (let's face it, you just can't go wrong with a giant crocodile). At the end of the day, it's probably the least painful *Highlander* movie. Nevertheless, when the Highlander's walking off into the sunset at the end and a seagull flies overhead, I was still praying that it would shit on him.

The Immortal Voyage of Captain Drake

(2009)

Directed by David Flores

Well, one thing is certain: whatever his captaining skills, with a name like "Drake" you know this guy can't rap.

So, I suppose it wouldn't have been very good marketing to call this movie "The *Chintzy* Voyage of Captain Drake", but it would've been a lot more accurate. The whole thing looks like an old Sinbad movie done on the cheap, except with cartoon monsters, and cartoon boats, and cartoon oceans, and cartoon buildings... Once again, I have to ask: why didn't they just make a goddamned cartoon? They probably would've saved a bundle too; I'm sure hiring voice actresses is way cheaper than hiring regular ones, because as long as they can speak clearly it doesn't even matter if they're fat. The story's some twaddle about finding the Tree of Life, as in the tree from the Bible that God doesn't wanting us meddling with. (It probably proves that he doesn't exist or something.) First stop, an old gravel pit, where everyone initially believes the Tree to be located (this must be that "sense of wonder" Steven Spielberg always aims for). Eventually though they learn that the Tree is actually hidden inside an iceberg at the North Pole, which seems somewhat more likely and does make for a slightly more epic quest. Not that it matters much, since the cast is so unenthusiastic about the whole deal you'd think they were standing in line to pay a library fine. For real, I've never seen people less excited to be chasing each across the globe or fighting to the death over the ultimate prize. I'm sorry if you're bored, actors, but you are drawing a paycheck here (probably), so I think you should at least *pretend* to make the effort. Then again, it's easy to understand their apathy once we finally see the "wondrous" Tree, in no small part because it's sporting this blatantly-artificial white coating that makes it look not unlike the little Xmas tree your grandmother used to display on her coffee table every year because a real tree wouldn't fit inside her apartment. Remember that thing? And how she'd spray that fake snow all over it that we later learned causes cancer? And then she died of cancer? Ah, memories.

Jack the Giant Killer

(1962)

Directed by Nathan Juran

It's the princess's birthday, and who should crash the party but the evil magician everyone hates but, apparently, no one recognizes. Just one of the many benefits of not having a Facebook page. The magician gives the princess a music box with a creepy dancing goblin inside, and no one thinks this is *too* weird until the little bastard pops out of his box while the princess is asleep, grows about twenty feet, and kidnaps her. It looks like she's fucked (metaphorically, I mean, but maybe literally too), until a random bystander steps up and manages to kill the giant goblin (jumbo shrimp) by going to town on it with a scythe. I'm betting this is Jack. The evil magician isn't through yet though, and even though he pronounces "coven" wrong (just like that lunkhead in *American Movie*) and his reasoning doesn't always make a whole lot of sense ("That illusion was merely to prove to you that I have her in reality." Your illusion proves in reality what now?), he does have a pretty big pair – strolling right into the king's chambers after kidnapping his daughter – not to mention a whole roomful of zombie-demons to back him up. (Why one of these zombie-demons is wearing a full-body bunny-rabbit costume, complete with ears, is a mystery though. Seriously, what the fuck?) The whole thing plays out like a cut-rate version of an old Sinbad movie, but rest assured I mean in the best possible way. Highlights include the giant goblin trashing a bunch of shit and getting his hand mashed by a millstone; a scene where a small child's father is killed right in front of him during an attack by flying, psychedelic witches; a truly boss cloak of invisibility effect; a leprechaun who only speaks in rhyme (okay, fine, he sucks); and some cool, bargain-basement giant monsters duking it out during the thrilling climax. Definitely worth a look-see.

Knight Chills

(2001)

Directed by Katherine Hicks

The only thing I can think of that's more lame and boring than playing Dungeons & Dragons is watching *other* people play Dungeons & Dragons, and fuck me sideways if that isn't exactly what this wretched movie is about. That's right, our main dweebs sit around playing D&D for nearly *half the fucking running time* before anything actually happens! *Finally* one of them commits suicide after being rejected by a chick (the fifth leading cause of death among D&D enthusiasts, right after shame), after which he returns from the grave as an evil, undead knight intent on killing everyone in his former gaming pod. Which comes as no surprise, since being murdered/possessed by evil spirits is the third leading cause of death among D&D enthusiasts. (For the record, number two is being attacked by a baboon while LARPing, and number one is diabetes-induced heart failure.) With a mentally unstable, supernatural knight on the loose I began to think that this movie might fail to disappoint after all, but as it turns out the murders are all completely low-key and mostly off-camera. Are you fucking kidding me??? Really, if you're gonna be that much of a pussy about it, why not have all the victims just die in their sleep or something? And I know that people who play this much Dungeons & Dragons generally don't get laid, but there had to be a way to work some some tits in here somewhere. Chicks have to shower sometime, right? This whole movie was fucking unbelievable. It's like the definition of weak.

Krull

(1983)

Directed by Peter Yates

Everyone who grew up in the 1980's remembers *Krull*, but no one can ever quite recall if they've actually seen it or not. If you're not entirely sure yourself, here's what happens:

A giant castle full of space dicks lands on Krull, a planet that's still thrashing around in the Dark Ages, or at least the Dark Ages as pictured by Hollywood executives whose entire grasp of the concept is based on some airbrushed artwork they once saw on the side of a van. The leader of the alien dicks organizes endless raiding parties that pillage and destroy to no stated purpose, which is tolerated by the locals to a surprising degree until they kidnap their mega-hot queen played by forgotten 1980's superbabe Lysette Anthony, who might just be the finest actress that a judge has ordered me not to come within 500 feet of. This absolutely will not stand, so our main guy tracks down this movie's answer to Excalibur, a magical sci-fi boomerang which he retrieves, bare-handed, right out of a pool of molten rock. And I will admit, watching this part legitimately made me cringe. Seriously, dude, next time just fish it out of there with a stick or something. Next our main guy rounds up a team of fellow adventurers to aid him in his dangerous quest, which if you ask me means that the survivors should *all* get a turn with the queen once they rescue her. Hey, they're risking their lives too, right? Main guys never seem to see it that way though. His cohorts are all annoying (the comedic relief wizard), clichés (*another* blind seer?), or annoying clichés (the honorable crooks), but the worst of all has to be the ridiculous-looking cyclops with his laughably tragic curse. See, the cyclops has the power to see into the future, but the only event he can clearly perceive is his own death. Wow, that's so deep, especially for a character with no depth perception. After various acts of derring-duh and challenges involving everything from a giant, translucent spider (admittedly cool) to quicksand (no, this isn't the one where the horse sinks in quicksand and your girlfriend cries, that's *The Neverending Story*), the main guy finally defeats the alien leader by utilizing the power of love. Plus the complimentary, and somewhat more effective, power of shooting fire out of his hands.

Remember it now? Yeah, me neither, and I just watched it thirty minutes ago.

The Last Unicorn

(1982)

Directed by Jules Bass and Arthur Rankin Jr.

The last unicorn in the world (who, I should note, is completely insufferable) learns from this unbelievably irritating butterfly (instantly the most obnoxious, rage-inducing animated character in the history of ever, and I'm including the GEICO gecko when I say that) that her horny brethren weren't wiped due to over-hunting or feudal sprawl after all. In fact, they're not even dead - they were just run out of town on a rail by something called the Red Bull, no doubt in the course of some Stratos style marketing gimmick.

Sounds like a quest to me.

Overall this movie is about as gay as you would expect a cartoon about unicorns to be, but the weird thing about it is that it's *obsessed* with tits: a vulture monster has a bunch of sloppy, used-up, single mom mams hanging out all over the place, and in another part a tree comes to life and buries this wizard's face in its own gigantic rack. Tits on a hot chick (or even a mediocre chick) are one thing, but I don't want my theoretical kids exposed to this creepy shit. And what's with the guys who offer the wizard a *taco?* What the fuck? As if the preceding isn't dumb enough, when the main unicorn finally tracks down her kinfolk she learns that an evil king has hidden them *underwater.* So... they've just been holding their breath this whole time? And don't even get me started on the nonsensical ending that features a skeleton getting drunk (how in the hell could a *skeleton* get drunk?), a guy with a sword going apeshit on a clock, millions of unicorns galloping out of the ocean, and an entire castle collapsing for absolutely no reason. It's completely retarded. To make things even worse, the soundtrack features songs by the band America, who always have and always will suck, just like most bands named after geographical locations. (Chicago, Boston, Europe, the Bay City Rollers... tell me I'm wrong.) In short, these clowns took a movie that should just be gay and boring and managed to make it gay, boring, disturbing, *and* ridiculous, with a shitty soundtrack. Nice job, dipshits.

Lord of the G-Strings

(2003)

Directed by Terry M. West

To be fair, the *Lord of the Rings* movies do have a lot going for them. They're long, they have lots of special effects, and they're based on literature and trust me movie critics eat that shit up. One thing they don't have though is Misty Mundae dyking it up with a hot redheaded barmaid, which means that this take is superior in at least one important aspect. (For those of you who aren't familiar with her, Misty Mundae is one of the hottest actresses ever, and if you don't want to fuck her you can just go ahead and tick "Become queer" off your bucket list because mission accomplished, buddy. And don't give me that "she's just not my type" business. If you aren't attracted to Misty Mundae, then your "type" is penis, period.) The story concerns an evil hottie who's defeated and stripped of her magical g-string; the farting, villainous bad guy who's after it; and a drunken wizard who enlists Misty and her dumb, slutty friends to deliver it to the volcano where it can finally be destroyed. Unfortunately for Misty, the forces of evil aren't too far behind ("I might have gotten drunk last night at a tavern and told several people," admits the wizard), and along the way she's also forced to deal with an appearance by the Cowardly Lion (what?), a (failed) attempt at Monty Python style humor via a non-stereotypically gay knight, and lots and lots of farting. I did like the hilarious anticlimax where the g-string is just casually handed off to some disinterested dude sitting in the volcano's basement, reading a magazine, but overall this is a pretty shitty movie. Farting isn't funny, and Misty spends more time with her clothes on than with them off, which is fine if you're, say, at church (I guess), but not so much if you're starring in pornography. I mean really, cute chicks wearing all their clothes? I've got the Disney Channel for that.

The Lords of Magick

(1989)

Directed by David Marsh

When someone spells "magic" with a "k" they're usually not talking about the cat who did card tricks at your thirteenth birthday party (you dork); they're talking about some seriously badass supernatural shit, and something pretty amazing is about to go down. Not this time though. An evil sorcerer kidnaps the local princess (and I don't blame him - nice fucking legs) and spirits her off to the future, or as we know it, regular times. Fortunately for her, two bozos, er, *heroic wizards* are hot on his trail, and they quickly hook up with this average Joe who helps them navigate the perils of 1989 in exchange for a primer in the dark arts. (You know every Dungeons & Dragons geek watching this stupid movie was all "Man that would be *so awesome!*" when the wizards put this offer on the table.) Epic quests to rescue leggy princesses held hostage in mysterious lands were fairly complicated endeavors back in the old magic-and-mead days (I know, because I've seen all the *Deathstalker* movies), but not anymore, apparently: these guys just drive their car to the house where the princess is being held and pick her up. Ah ha ha ha ha ha ha! That's ridiculous. Of course the evil sorcerer comes after them, leading to a climactic battle in a big warehouse full of empty boxes, which I assume was available because the cop show that was supposed to be shooting there wrapped early that day. As a general rule, most audiences expect fantasy movies like this to be heavy on the dragons and monsters and topless chicks with swords, and pretty light on the cardboard boxes. These guys have it all mixed up. Jackasses.

MacGyver: "Good Knight MacGyver"

(1991)

Directed by Michael Vejar

In this episode, MacGyver, the guy who can use high school science and dodgy writing to build almost anything out of the most basic materials, is hit in the head by a falling flowerpot (I swear) and wakes up in the days of King Arthur, a famous historical personage who didn't actually exist. He uses a lasso to win a jousting contest, repeatedly punks Merlin the Magician, impresses the yokels with a match (a trope so played-out that even a Martin Lawrence movie effectively mocked it), escapes a deathtrap with the help of a corkscrew, builds an impromptu dog whistle (give me a fucking break), and flies a kite during a thunderstorm, all in the course of pacifying the Knights of the Round Table (portrayed here as a bunch of easily-manipulated hotheads) and, later, rescuing a ~~beautiful~~ maiden from the evil Morgana, who's invented gunpowder a few centuries early in a bid to control all trade routes to China. Morgana's second is skeletonized after falling into molten lava, there's a brief dungeon crawl complete with a death trap and a monster (okay, fine, it's just a dog, but I'm pretty sure "Dog" is an entry in the *Monster Manual*, right?), and MacGyver explains to Merlin why he shouldn't be drinking alcohol while on a long hike, a bit that also appears in a contemporary (late 1990) episode of *Star Trek: The Fake Generation*. Since Paramount television produced both these shows, I can only assume that one of the writers there at the time was either a militant teetotaler, or just incredibly lazy. After watching "Good Knight MacGyver", my money's on lazy.

Masters of the Universe

(1987)

Directed by Gary Goddard

Okay, no one can deny that the He-Man/Masters of the Universe cartoon promoted an enormous, throbbing, pro-gay agenda, which is fine because it was right out there in the open and it's not like they were trying to bullshit anybody. The live-action version, on the other hand, was made under completely different circumstances by a completely different studio with completely different priorities, so I'm gonna do my best to ignore the homo angle and review this movie on its own terms.

This movie sucks.

First and foremost, is the "wacky" dwarf really necessary? There was no toy of this guy and he wasn't in the cartoon, so why do we have to put up with his ass-sucking antics here? And what the fuck happened to Skeletor? Even though you knew he just got done falling down the stairs with a bucket on his head, in the cartoon he still *looked* reasonably badass, but the movie version looks like something you'd throw together an hour before the costume party because your girlfriend just informed you that it *is* a costume party and you did the "To: Women, From: God" thing last year. (By the way, you're a douche.) Seriously, if I picked up the Skeletor mask used in this movie in the Walgreen's Halloween aisle I'd be reasonably satisfied, but this is a ~~big budget~~ Hollywood movie for God's sake and the slipshod approach they took here really isn't cutting it. Of course the story is retarded beyond words: we open on a planet that looks like deleted scenes from *Krull*, but most of the action goes down on Earth because when it comes to cheap location shooting, nothing beats the Earth. He-Man and the rest of the good guys end up here first, but when they lose their teleportation gizmo this kid finds it, decides it's "one of those new Japanese synthesizers" (Jesus Christ kill me now) and tries to rock out with it, which alerts the bad guys to their location. This leads to an enormous sci-fi battle: we've got spaceships flying around, buildings and cars exploding, bodies strewn all over Main Street... *Absolutely no one notices any of this though*. Even when the cops do show up they completely dismiss the sole person who reported it and suggest that he just needs to "get a little rest"! Seriously, the amount of contempt this piece of fucking shit has for the people watching it boggles the fucking mind. Fuck you too, assholes. From top to bottom, the sole person involved in the production of this epic turd who got it right was the one who cast the chicks: Evil-Lyn is hot enough to give the Pope wet dreams, Teela has an ass that could cut butter (no, as a matter of fact I *don't* know what I mean by that), and hungry hungry Courteney Cox is on hand too and since this was made back in her pre-anorexia, pre-hag days even she's looking pretty tasty. Too bad we never see a single one of these women naked. There is a scene with a shirtless man in bondage though. Honestly, I don't know why I expected anything else from *He-Man*.

Mazes and Monsters

(1982)

Directed by Steven Hilliard Stern

Mazes and Monsters was originally a novel, written to cash in on the early 1980's "Dungeons & Dragons will make you commit suicide" scare, and people who are into Dungeons & Dragons are still pretty bitter about it, as evidenced by all the negative reviews it has on Amazon even though it really is an okay book. The movie version is one of several "one way or another, Dungeons & Dragons *will* kill you" flicks that came out about this time – other examples being *The Dungeonmaster* (covered in my book *66.6 Absurd Movies About the Devil*) and *Skullduggery* (1983) – and whereas the book was kind of sad and actually made you feel sorry for the main guy, in the movie he's played by Mr. for-your-Oscar-consideration himself Forrest Gump, so watching him lose his mind and become a pious 10th level cleric who forsakes pussy, hallucinates Gorn attacks, and has weird, low-rent dreams wherein a back-lit guy dressed like me says cryptic things to him from the far end of a storm tunnel is less tragic and more endlessly hilarious. What finally pushes him over the edge (you might what to make a note of this) is when they decide to play ~~Dungeons & Dragons~~ Mazes and Monsters "live" in some nearby caverns, and points for realism because crawling around an unlit cave in full Renaissance faire gear looks about as much fun here as it probably would be in real life. They keep at it though (the nerd gene is a stubborn gene), right up until Forrest disappears and the police get involved:

NERD: "What do you guys think happened?"

DETECTIVE: "One of the players Robbie played with... got carried away and killed him."

NERD: "Well, that's kind of far out...."

DETECTIVE: "Mazes and Monsters is a far-out game."

Forrest/Robbie isn't dead though, he's in New York, where, after surviving an attack by punk rockers (when people in the early 1980's weren't wringing their hands over Dungeons & Dragons, they were generally wringing their hands over punk rock), he has a moment of clarity and calls his friends, who show up just in time to prevent him from leaping off the World Trade Center. Nevertheless, in the end he remains completely untethered from reality, the ultimate fate of anyone foolhardy enough to play Dungeons & and Dragons, or any of its knock-off equivalents. I hear Bunnies & Burrows is a safe alternative though.

Merlin and the Sword

(1985)

Directed by Clive Donner

Back in the early 1980's the movie *Excalibur* was quite popular, even though nobody really liked it or actually bothered to see it. A ripoff was inevitable, and here it is. It starts when this broad visiting Stonehenge falls into a hole and meets Merlin the Magician, who's been imprisoned in a cave beneath the place for centuries. Eager to bore her with his story, Merlin uses his magical powers to open a window to the past, which is where the bulk of ~~the action~~ this movie goes down:

It's the time of Camelot (Arthur's, not Kennedy's) (and not Arthur Kennedy's), and everything's hunky-dory until King Arthur's wife is queen-napped. Some of his knights go looking for her, and Art makes like he's gonna be right behind them – just tying his shoelaces, you know – but instead he just wanders around for a while and then goes back to the castle. Well played, your majesty. Meanwhile, Morgan le Fay (who has hair straight out of a 1980's Heart video, except somehow worse) is contriving all these ridiculous plans to defeat Arthur, my favorite being when she slaps a suit of armor on a high school science lab skeleton and calls it an "undead knight". ("He's going to fight... *that?*" says her nephew. My sentiments exactly.) And what is Merlin doing this whole time? Well, in one part he impresses his way into a chick's pants by performing card tricks. If I saw a cat try this in real life you couldn't pay me to not kick his ass, and now I've just dropped good cash money to watch it happen in a goddamned movie. And I guess the chick in question agrees with me, because she's the one who ultimately seals Merlin in that cave for 1000 years. There's also a girl who looks like a pig but transforms into a hottie after someone marries her (wow, it's the exact opposite of real life), and a fight between Lancelot and an absurd dragon (special effects courtesy the 1940's) that he's well on his way to losing until Merlin travels back in time and rescues him. Which makes absolutely no sense whatsoever, because if Merlin can travel through time why didn't he do so ages ago and fix everything that led to his imprisonment in the first place? Oh, wait, someone later explains that he *didn't have the time*. Seriously, fuck this movie.

Fun Fact: Looks like the techno band Lords of Acid snagged the line "She has the body of a woman, she has the power to bewitch" (from "Voodoo U") directly from this flick. I'm pretty sure I'm the first person to figure this out, so I'll be expecting some kind of award.

The Norseman

(1978)

Directed by Charles B. Pierce

A bunch of vikings, led by the Six Million Dollar Man, sail to the United States of America to spring their buddies, who've been captured by Indians (casino, not 7-11). Like the vast majority of their ilk (notable exceptions: Tonto, Pocahontas, the Cleveland Indian) these Indians are irredeemably evil, so it's no surprise that they captured the first group of vikings by pretending to be their friends and then dry-gulching them when they least expected it. Every time someone in this movie opens their mouth they say something irredeemably stupid ("No one had ever seen his face..." while we're looking right at the guy's face; a Viking tells an Indian "I know you don't understand what I'm saying," and then asks her a bunch of questions), but I'm more than willing to let that slide because let's face it, vikings vs. Indians is an *awesome* idea. It's like something a small child would come up with, and for my money Hollywood could do a lot worse than hitting up small children for their movie ideas in exchange for, say, a full college scholarship (at a state school, of course) or all the candy they can eat in one sitting, their choice. I'd really like to see more movies where they mix it up like this, like maybe viking vs.

ninjas, or army guys vs. knights, or even cowboys vs. Eskimos. For real, I'll watch anything like this that they can come up with.

The Odyssey

(1987)

Written by Homer

This animated movie chronicles the adventures of ancient rhyming mariner Odysseus, who, they say, once infiltrated an enemy city by hiding inside a giant wooden horse. Truth be told, I never bought that yarn. I mean really, who would fall for something like that? And even if they were that clueless, who sees a giant wooden horse parked outside their crib and is all like "You know, that could be useful. We better bring it inside before some kids swipe it or something." What the hell did they even plan on doing with it? I'm sorry, but the whole story is pretty suspect. Fortunately *The Odyssey* is primarily about Odysseus's journey home following the horse incident, and all the grief his crew is handed along the way. Not that I'm too surprised, considering his second-in-command is named "You Lick Us". Every time that guy introduces himself is just another excuse for someone to start a fight with them.

Actually, the trouble really begins when they stop to score some grub and are captured by a cyclops. Inexplicably, the cyclops's next move is to get completely skunked, so after he passes out Odysseus puts his eye out. Blind, drunk, and stupid isn't much of a combination, so the sailors easily escape, but it turns out that the cyclops's dad is a fucking god (nice one, idiots) who, thoroughly pissed, blows their ship so far off course that it'll take them *years* to get home. (Savvy readers may notice that this entire premise was ripped off wholesale by *Star Trek: Voyager*, widely regarded by me to be the third worst Star Trek series of them all. Even adding that hottie 60 of 9 wasn't enough to get me to watch that tiresome crap.) Fortunately our heroes are subsequently able to confer with this witch, and she tells Odysseus to go to Hell. I don't mean she tells him to fuck off, I mean the actual place, where he's to speak with this specific ghost who can at least tell them how to overcome the many challenges that lie ahead. Odysseus gets the 411, escapes Hell by punking this movie's bargain-basement three-headed dog that only has two heads, and the running of the gauntlet commences.

The first challenge: evil mermaids whose song is said to be so alluring (even better than Ke$ha) that men are drawn right to the bitches, who then eat them. And after that they *still* expect child support. Our heroes stymie the mermaids by plugging their ears with wax, but they're not missing much because we do get to hear their song and frankly it sounds like Shonen Knife, played backwards, and at the wrong speed. The sailors manage to overcome the next few challenges too, but when they visit this island where they're forbidden to kill any animals an adorable little baby cow comes rolling up with the big Bambi eyes and shit and really, you just *have* to kill an irritating fucker like that. So they do, and all hell breaks loose. The captain of the gods pops a gasket, nukes their entire boat, and the only one who survives is Odysseus.

Odysseus eventually washes ashore and meets a princess, but then, just his luck, she's set to be sacrificed to the cyclops's dad, the very god who started all this trouble in the first place. Our hero has had just about enough by this point, so when the god shows up to collect Odysseus jumps him, and, not unlike a leprechaun, once captured the god is forced to grant him two wishes. Odysseus wishes for an end to the human sacrifices and for the god to get off his fucking back, the god makes it so, and everyone lives happily ever after, the end. Now, I didn't think this sounded right at all, so I went back to the original source (*Clash of the Titans*) and I was correct - the original ending is completely different. It's still an okay cartoon though, and I really liked the quiz they included as a DVD bonus. Here's a real question they ask, and the real multiple-choice answers:

9. Scylla and Charybdis are:

> A. a comedy team
> B. a law firm
> C. a many-headed monster and a whirlpool
> D. Odysseus' in-laws

A smart-assed quiz may seem like a lame DVD extra to some, but if you ask me it's infinitely more entertaining than watching some dullard actor flub his lines fifty goddamned times in a row. "Ha ha! He messed up again! What an asshole!" Seriously, DVD producers, we are so over that shit.

Pegasus vs. Chimera

(2012)

Directed by John Bradshaw

This evil king wants to wipe out the few remaining pockets of hating his puke-soaked guts, so he enlists a chimera, a monster that's half lion, half serpent, and half goat. (Source: "Monster" Manuel, my Hispanic mythology expert.) To counter this, the good guys summon Pegasus the winged horse, but this movie is so goddamned chintzy that their winged horse *doesn't even have any wings*. Well, that's not entirely true; on the few occasions when Pegasus is actually flying around some cartoon wings do spontaneously materialize, but when the good guys are grounded or just walking someplace (which is most of the time), the wings mysteriously vanish. Okay, really, why would you make a Pegasus movie about a (practically) wingless Pegasus??? That's what makes him fucking Pegasus, and not, say, My Friend Flicka, or... what was that show with the talking horse? Oh yeah, *Sex and the City*. And why are the good guys walking anywhere anyway? *They have a flying horse.* Jesus fucking H., get a clue, people. I swear to Bubo, if I ever teach a course called "How Not to Make a Pegasus Movie" I'm gonna show this piece of shit on the first day, send everyone home, and spend the rest of the semester smoking weed in my office. Office hours will be 2-6 PM Monday and Wednesday, in case any co-eds need some additional face time. BYOB.

Prisoners of the Lost Universe

(1983)

Directed by Terry Marcel

Everybody falls into an off-brand Stargate and, ironically enough, lands in that vacant lot behind K-Mart where 90% of the *Stargate* TV series actually took place. The group's only female is immediately chicknapped by the locals, so Richard Hatch (*Battlestar Galactica*; endless embarrassing attempts to revive *Battlestar Galactica*) goes after them and has numerous adventures that can best be described as "incomprehensible". There's cavemen, a green dude who looks like the Orion slave girl's nerd brother, and even some A-rabs, proving once and for all that Islam is the one true religion in any and all dimensions, even totally absurd ones. Praise Allah! Eventually the good guys raid the chief bad guy's fortress and we've got bombs going off and fools flying through the air and the whole thing has blown so far past ridiculous that they'd have to make a u-turn and drive for hours just to get back to the place where ridiculous began. The absolute dumbest thing about this flick though is the jaw-droppingly stupid effect they repeatedly break out when someone gets punched. See, as soon as the punch connects, the scene briefly rewinds and then we see the same punch connect again! I guess this is supposed to make it look like two punches were landed in rapid succession, but in practice it looks more like someone accidentally sat on the remote. There's no gore, no tits, and even when something interesting does go down, like the scene where this hottie is lashed with a whip, it's completely off-camera so we can't even see it! What a load of ass. Seriously, it's a good thing my time isn't valuable, because watching this anal turkey baster would've been a tragic waste of it.

The Raiders of Atlantis

(1983)

Directed by Ruggero Deodato

People who believe Atlantis was a real place (these people usually smell like patchouli) generally portray it as a peaceful land of magic and wonder, filled with amazing, super-advanced technology powered entirely by rainbows and clean-burning unicorn farts. When Atlantis actually does rise from the sea though, the people in this movie learn the brutal truth: it was really run by punk rock bikers who sole goal in this life or any other is to kick the ever-loving shit out of everybody. They start by invading the closest island (on motorcycles, of course), where they trash everything in sight and kill anyone and everyone who crosses their path. A few people do manage to escape though, and as it turns out a couple of them are some pretty bad motherfuckers. The main guy, for example, is so chill and jaded that when he learns Atlantis has returned and that the undying Atlanteans plan on taking over the entire world, his only reaction is "Crap!" Our main cats quickly organize the survivors, and they engage in a violent running battle with the Atlanteans, both sides hitting the other with everything they've got, including guns, axes, swords, flamethrowers, and Molotov cocktails. And of course the good guys pull the old "decapitating a biker by stringing wire across the road" gag.

Eventually some of our heroes manage to escape in a helicopter, but instead of heading for the hills they decide to – thank you, truth in advertising – *raid Atlantis*. Atlantis proper turns out to be pretty underwhelming, but you just can't argue with a movie called "Raiders of Atlantis" that actually delivers, even if it is kind of ridiculous and the end is completely incomprehensible. Totally recommended.

Useful Fact: Chicks who believe in Atlantis tend to be pretty easy.

Riverworld

(2003)

Directed by Kari Skogland

The Space Shuttle explodes [insert tasteless Challenger joke here], but instead of being reduced to a fine mist that burns up in the atmosphere, the sole astronaut on board finds himself washing up on the shore of a mysterious river, naked and covered with sperm. Welcome to South Africa! Ha ha! Several more naked people climb out of the river too, but the shore is littered with thermoses full of clothing so in short order each and every one of them is ready for tea with the Queen and we never see even a single tit. And speaking of tea, their next discovery is a gigantic machine that provides free food, although no one thinks to ask for something that's been discontinued (like, say, Keebler Cheeblers, or Monster Chomps brand cookies), so I'm not exactly sure what, if any, limitations it might have. The whole setup seems benign enough (I mean, free clothes, free food... it's either Heaven or the liberals are in office again), although at least one of the river people, a caveman, is even more confused and hostile than the audience should be at this point and ends up initiating a ruckus. Soon everyone is captured by barbarians, they befriend an alien who has Parkinson's disease, a mysterious magical figure helps them escape from the barbarians, and eventually they hook up with a second group that plans on exploring the mysterious river in a boat from Tom Sawyer days. They need a meteorite to power this boat though, so they enlist the astronaut to go back and steal one from the barbarians, because of course the barbarians have a riverboat-powering meteorite. The good guys are betrayed by one of their own though, so the barbarians capture everybody (again), leading to a climactic battle featuring swordplay and kung fu.

Who comes up with this shit?

The Runestone

(1991)

Directed by Willard Carroll

An ancient viking runestone is unearthed, and I'll be damned if somebody in the prop department didn't sneak the word "fuck" onto it. (To see this for yourself, visit my blog at mrsatanism.blogspot.com[1] and search for entries tagged "trash of the titans".) A viking runestone expert is on the case, but this old harbinger dude warns him that the stone will try to use "what you want most" against him. And I guess what he wants most is to change into a werewolf, chase his ex-girlfriend all over town, and kill everyone he crosses paths with along the way, because in short order that's exactly what happens. Eventually several disparate people decide to get to the bottom of this nonsense, including a cop (who we know we're supposed to like, because he's addicted to Pez and keeps Godzilla toys on his desk. He's quirky.), a kid, two old geezers, a Swede... Truth be told, there were so many goofballs in on this business that I lost track of who they all were. With this much potential fodder on hand you'd think the monster would thin out their ranks at least a little bit before the final credit roll, but most of them ultimately survive which is pretty weak if you ask me. Eventually the good guys learn that it all has something to do

---

1. http://mrsatanism.blogspot.com/

with "Ragnarok", which if you've ever read the Marvel comic book *Thor* you know is the viking version of the apocalypse. Of course in the Thor comics Ragnarok went down approximately every nine issues or so, so after a while it turned into kind of a joke, and let's face it, it's pretty much a joke here too. I mean really, it's *one werewolf chasing his ex around.* How do movies always manage to make the end of the world so trite? On the plus side, the werewolf does kill a *lot* of people, even if the vast majority of them are peripheral. (The scene where he busts up this hotel and slaughters a shitload of cops in the process is particularly awesome.) There's a huge fight at the end that makes almost no sense (why, exactly, do they go to another planet?), but given the overall body count they rack up I'm willing to cut the people who made this flick a little slack. They really should've cast more women though; the only one on hand is stunningly mediocre, and she never even takes her clothes off. I think we can all agree that an apocalypse without naked chicks is an apocalypse most of us can afford to miss.

Samson

(1961)

Directed by Gianfranco Parolini

Muscle-bound homo Samson is hunting boar with his buddies when he crosses wires with another meathead who starts giving him lip. They decide to fight, and for the next few minutes we're basically watching pro wrestling, except even gayer which until now I didn't think was even possible. But before they reach the inevitable conclusion of this battle – where they collapse, exhausted, into each others beefy arms and make sweet, sweet, ass love – some soldiers appear and Samson and his pals (I swear one of them is Norberg from *Police Squad!*) are arrested. The soldiers try to put them in jail, but Samson keeps tearing the cell door off and beating people with it (seriously, this happens at least twice), and he pulls plenty of other tough-guy shit too, like lifting a gigantic manhole cover, ripping a stump in half with his bare hands, and pulling a whole goddamn building down on some fools. He never takes the next logical step and just starts tearing people's arms and heads off though, which would've made his job a lot easier while simultaneously making this movie a lot more entertaining. The thing that really irritated me about this flick though was how vague it was about the bad guy's final fate. Could someone else who's seen this please tell me what, exactly, was supposed to be happening after he fell in the drink? I *think* a fish ate him, but I rewound it a couple of times and I'll be damned if I can tell for sure. I realize that a giant fish puppet was probably out of the producers' price range, but at the very least couldn't they have had him yell "Oh, shit! A giant fish! Help! Oh fuck!" or something? Just so it's clear what's going down? Really, how hard would that have been?

Samson and the 7 Miracles of the World

(1961)

Directed by Riccardo Freda

See Samson make his big entrance wearing a red diaper! See Samson pull an entire tree out of the ground! See Samson beat up a guy... with another guy! See Samson fight a hilariously fake stuffed tiger! See Samson settle a bar fight by pulling down the entire bar! See Samson do the *Raiders of the Lost Ark* under-the-truck scene with a chariot! See Samson knock *himself* unconscious while sounding the signal to start the big uprising! See Sampson start an earthquake after he's buried alive! See Samson kill the hottest chick in the entire movie, completely by accident!

Ha ha! Fucking brilliant. This movie rocks.

The Secret of NIMH

(1982)

Directed by Don Bluth

Why do so many cartoons portray nuisance vermin as lovable and/or heroic? Mice, rabbits, rats, yippy little dogs... why don't they make a cartoon about a tapeworm while they're at it? Or a liver fluke? I'd like to see you pull that one off, Disney: *Lester the Liver Fluke*. Good luck getting an Oscar nod for anything off *that* soundtrack. This cartoon features a family of mice who currently live inside an old cinder block (swank), but they have to clear out every spring before the farmer plows the field where the cinder block is located, and this year there's a problem: one of the baby mice is sick and he can't be moved. Okay, I'll be 100% honest here: I was rooting for the baby mouse to die. Seriously, how is that worse than him surviving, only to move into your house and surreptitiously poop in the Cocoa Krispies? Seriously, as soon as this cartoon is over I'm driving to the store and buying some extra traps. The painful, inhumane kind. Fucking mice.

So anyway, mama mouse goes to the local rats for help (apparently rats are like the 18th-Level Magic Users of the pest world), and as it turns out they used to roll with her husband so they're more then happy to lend a hand. Paw. They construct a complicated pulley system and lift the entire cinder block right out of the ground, but then one of the rats betrays everyone and drops the whole megilla right on their rat wizard's head. A rat sword fight breaks out, but the treacherous rat buys the ghost when a heroic rat hurls a knife right into his back, full-on ninja-style. Of course the cinder block is still stuck in the ground, now with *all* of the disease-carrying mouse children trapped inside, but fortunately for them (if not us) mom mouse uses this magic medallion provided by the rats to levitate the entire block to safety, kind of like Yoda did with Luke Skywalker's spaceship in *The Empire Strikes Back*, except in that case we knew Yoda could do things like that and they weren't just completely pulling it out of their ass. And really, since the medallion can do the job so easily, why didn't they just use it to move the block in the first place and forgo building the pulley system entirely, saving themselves endless shitloads of trouble? Seriously, the word "retarded" doesn't even begin to cover this movie. What a brainless piece of crap.

The mouse mom is pretty hot, though. If I was a mouse, I'd fuck her.

The 7 Adventures of Sinbad

(2010)

Directed by Ben Hayflick and Adam Silver

After a half-hearted gunfight, some modern-day pirates manage to seize an oil tanker in broad daylight, and while I don't want to sound unsympathetic here, I'm thinking that maybe the oil tanker guys could have reacted just a *little* sooner when they saw that small, open boat full of gun-toting, masked men heading straight for them. Seriously, a few well-aimed shots while the pirates were still several hundred yards out would've ended the whole thing right there. Also, isn't this supposed to be a Sinbad movie? Oh, I see, this time around Sinbad the Sailor is a modern-day businessdude. Because that's not ass-plumbingly stupid. Sinbad's company owns the oil tanker in question, so, just like any important, high-powered executive would do, he finds himself a gun and flies out there to handle this shit personally. He doesn't quite get to live out his Jean Clod Von Dim action fantasy though, because, wouldn't you know it, a giant squid suddenly shows up and sinks the tanker right out from under everybody.

Okay, what the hell? For real, is somebody fucking with me here? Is this that Justin French asshole again?

So now Sinbad's helicopter is crashing into the sea, and the next thing you know he washes ashore on this mysterious island where he's immediately mugged by a giant crab. This turns out to be one of those foreshadowing things, because after Sinbad locates the survivors from the downed oil tanker, they all spend the next several minutes fighting and/or running away from additional monsters. Mostly running away. Eventually they're captured by this militia group, there's a big gunfight, and nearly everyone chomps it, leaving only Sinbad and a chick sporting the tits of an undernourished ten-year-old boy. (Full disclosure: I'd still hit it.) They proceed to blow up a demon with high explosives, and then crash a hot-air balloon into the ocean where they're picked up by a passing ship. Now it's time to save the world (which is ending, for some damned reason), so Sinbad commandeers a mini-sub, befriends the giant squid I mentioned earlier, and then raises the sunken oil tanker, which fixes everything via the magic of this script was written by stool-hurling retards.

Seriously, how is this in any way a Sinbad movie? Fuck off.

Shakma

(1990)

Directed by Tom Logan and Hugh Parks

The college professor in this flick is conducting aggression experiments on baboons, hosts live-action Dungeons & Dragons games in deserted buildings, and keeps a Ouija board in his office. He's just begging to be a horror movie statistic. So what ultimately does him in? As it turns out, the baboon, which escapes and goes on a rampage during one of his LARP sessions. Of the potential victims, the only one worth rooting for is 1980's megababe Ari Meyers (AKA the brunette daughter from *Kate & Allie*), looking finger-lickin' good as the little princess the others are supposed to "rescue". The rest of them are idiots to the core, like the default main chick who, knowing full well that hurled shit is currently hitting the fan, has the black guy on the horn for a solid minute before she even *implies* that there might be an emergency situation afoot, and by then he's already figured it out for himself via a face full of pissed-off monkey. Stupid fucking twat. As far as I'm concerned, justice was served – with two free sides and your choice of dessert – when the monkey subsequently slaughtered her in a toilet stall. I hope the last thing she ever saw was someone's unflushed turd. And then there's the main guy... what is with this freak? Every dead body he finds is meticulously carried off and carefully stored in the same room, and while I can understand saving Ari Meyer's body for later (especially if it's still warm), overall this serves no practical purpose whatsoever, other than giving him repeated opportunities to act like a huge drama queen, which of course is exactly what he does. Naturally this movie breaks out a cheap-scare cat in a place where no cat should logically be, but infinitely worse is the *mouse* that somehow jumps five feet into the fucking air and lands on the main guy's shoulder to provide us with an additional, even stupider, cheap scare. Seriously, genetically-altered super mouse, maybe *you* could kill the baboon for them.

As you can see this isn't exactly *Monkey Shines* (1988), or even *In the Shadow of Kilimanjaro* (1986), but a good 60% of this movie consists of a (real) baboon repeatedly hurling itself into doors, which gets to be pretty funny after a while, and I also enjoyed the parts where it trashes a computer and, later, an entire laboratory. (This leads me to wonder what, exactly, one does with a baboon after it's been specifically trained to wreck shit, chase bad actors, and throw itself into things. I'll bet that poor bastard went on a one-way trip to the bottom of the river the instant this production wrapped.) The kills are passably bloody, one sap gets a face full of acid, and the way the baboon is ultimately dealt with is suitably inventive, ridiculous, gruesome, and hilarious. In short, if you think "kids play D&D and get attacked by a killer baboon" sounds like a good idea, you will probably like this movie.

Sinbad and the Minotaur

(2011)

Directed by Karl Zwicky

I've seen some stupid-ass movies in my time (example: *Van Helsing*), but 2010's *The 7 Adventures of Sinbad* was so fucking cretinous and nonsensical that I'm convinced the sole creative force behind it was Shakma, who wrote the script by flinging his poop at it. Because of this, I was really in the mood to cut *Sinbad and the Minotaur* some slack, and it gets off to a good start, with a suitably epic introduction that fills in the backstory whilst simultaneously acknowledging the role the gods inevitably play in tales like this. When you're making a movie about mythological shit, it's always good to start off with a little nod to the gods. They like that.

The story proper begins when Sinbad finds (by which I mean steals) an ancient scroll that reveals the location of a gigantic, solid gold head, and before long he and his crew are off to swipe the damn thing. Now, movies about epic quests share one very important aspect with college road trip movies, and that is this: the best part of any epic quest, or college road trip, is always what happens *en route*. After all, it took a long time to get from point A to point B in Sinbad days, and there were always endless amazing adventures to be had and tons of cool-ass monsters to fight along the way. Not like today, when it's mostly just strip malls and Burger Kings. This movie though skips the voyage entirely and jumps right to the point where our heroes arrive at their final destination! Way to completely miss the point, idiots. Seriously, if any movie in history could have actually benefited by trotting out an endless parade of cartoon monsters, this is the one, but the minotaur is pretty much the whole show here, and frankly he's not that impressive. It's all so fucking phoned-in, but at least the story makes sense, and the featured chicks are exceptionally hot, even by exceptionally hot standards. (It's a pity that the standout, even among them, gets tortured to death.) I also liked the main bad guy - the big speech he gives regarding his plans for the gold is surprisingly badass. In fact, it would probably go down as a classic movie villain speech, if it were only in a movie anyone actually cared to watch.

Sinbad: Legend of the Seven Seas

(2003)

Directed by Patrick Gilmore and Tim Johnson

Why are Sinbad movies always full of Greek monsters? Sure, the siren sequence in this cartoon features one of the coolest takes on sirens I've ever seen (they're made of water and when you fuck them, you drown), but shouldn't Sinbad be fighting Arabian monsters? Then again, in one of the classic Sinbad movies he fought a giant fucking walrus, so I suppose it could be worse. That aside, this is a really good cartoon - there's plenty of adventure, the jokes are actually funny, the comedic relief dog behaves like a real dog instead of a dog in a cartoon, and the main chick is pretty fine, even if she does turn out to be a total whore. I also liked it when our heroes reached the end of the world: in this movie the Earth is so flat that even the chick from *The 7 Adventures of Sinbad* wouldn't be jealous, but instead of flowing over the side, the water at the edge of the world is *evaporating*. Up instead of down: how deceptively simple, conceptually, yet infinitely cool is that? It just goes to show how fucking lazy most movies really are. Cartoon or no, this entry definitely ranks as one of the best Sinbad movies ever made. The only part I didn't like was when the goddess Eris got punked, but that's only because I used to be a Discordian before I became Miley Cyrus to a banana jackalope.

Sinbad of the Seven Seas

(1989)

Directed by Enzo G. Castellari

A woman who, we'll soon learn, is hopelessly fried on on some pretty serious drugs, or possibly just insane, tells her daughter a bedtime story about Sinbad. It begins with Sinbad (played by the Incredible Hulk) and his five sailor friends, resplendent in their purple spandex and jewelry that Liberace rejected as being too gaudy, returning home from a long, hard, veiny voyage at sea. Once there though, they discover that the place has completely gone to shit: this prick of a wizard has taken over the entire city ("My extraordinary powers make me top of the heap around here!" he explains), and he captures Sinbad and throws him into the dungeon, which, in an added supervillain bonus, is crawling with snakes. Sinbad commiserates with the snakes though, and when they realize that he feels their pain they let him tie several of them together into a rope which he uses to escape. He quickly rounds up his faggot crew, and they all sail off in search of these magical gems that can purportedly destroy the wizard once and for all. (Initially we're told that there are seven of these gems, but later someone says that there are only four, and ultimately I think they actually end up with five. Hey, moviemaking is easy. It's counting that's hard.) Naturally each of the gems is stashed in a dangerous, inaccessible place where adventures are required to retrieve it. One is located on the Island of the Dead, for example. Another is being held by the Amazon Queen, who, they say, is so beautiful that no man can resist her (obviously not an issue for Sinbad's crew). Okay, I've read all the Sinbad stories, and I don't remember any of this shit. Seriously, makers of this movie, if you just wanted to make up a Sinbad adventure from scratch, why not drop the "deranged bedtime story" angle entirely so you could include some some decent gore and/or naked Muslim chicks? Or hell, keep it kiddie-friendly if you want; I'd settle for a couple of scenes that make sense and/or don't completely suck.

For real, this is a total pile. Recommended for fags who have a crush on the Hulk only.

Sinbad the Sailor

(1947)

Directed by Richard Wallace

There's basically two kinds of Sinbad movies: the kind full of amazing monsters and swashbuckling adventure (*Sinbad: Legend of the Seven Seas*; *The Golden Voyage of Sinbad*), and the kind where Sinbad swishes around like a tenth-generation fag and they treat the whole production like an enormous joke that you're not in on (*Sinbad of the Seven Seas*; *Son of Sinbad*). This one falls somewhere in the middle. In the plus column we've got a whole shipload of sailors who kick off after drinking the green Kool-Aid, Sinbad testing his drinking water for poison by giving it to the laziest member of his crew, and a part where Sinbad tricks some soldiers into sliding off a roof, assumedly to their deaths although this is unconfirmed. On the other hand: talk talk talk talk talk talk talk. Is it too much to ask that an adventure movie shut the fuck up long enough to have some goddamned adventure in it? I've seen Kevin Smith flicks that didn't rely so much on over-written blathering. In fact, this movie is almost nothing but talk until the very end, when Sinbad finally lands on this mysterious island that's bursting from the rafters with treasure, only to ultimately learn that the *real* treasure is *love*. Of course he keeps all the gold he finds there too. Say what you will about the man, he's not an idiot.

Skullduggery

(1983)

Directed by Ota Richter

Our main guy is prompted to kill randoms by an ancient curse, represented at various times by a guy in a dark, smokey room assembling a puzzle recommended for ages retarded and under; a gay, two-bit magician; and a creepy jester doll. He gets his cues as to who, specifically, he should off though from the non-infringing Dungeons & Dragons knockoff he's been playing with his friends. It certainly *sounds* like a horror movie, and the horror parts are at least semi-serious, but it also features anything-goes style gags à la *Airplane!*; endless WTF moments (a doctor casually wandering around the hospital in a gorilla suit, banging nurses); weird, jokey fakeouts (the main guy tries to kill a chick and hits her reflection in a mirror instead; he thinks he's being arrested, but it's just a cop show on TV); lots of homosexual references (including an utterly random cameo by a Liberace proxy, and a dude dressed as a gay stereotype take on Alex from *A Clockwork Orange*); inexplicable bunny imagery; a running tic-tac-toe gag with no payoff because, apparently, no one involved with this production understood how tic-tac-toe is actually played; a part where the main guy effortlessly picks up a hot, horny nurse like so many American werewolves in London before him; and cluelessly idiotic exchanges like this:

TAROT READER: "Your father's name was... Jeremy"

MAIN GUY: "How did you know that? He's been dead for 18 years."

The main guy's killing spree culminates at this weird Hellfire Club-esque costume party full of people swapping 1980's T&A comedy gags ("Could you please deflate your tits?") while everyone dances to the movie's theme song, which couldn't possibly be more inappropriate for dancing to. The very last shot is someone flipping us off.

Pretty much mandatory viewing.

Solomon Kane

(2009)

Directed by Michael J. Bassett

There's a lot of shit the history books gloss over, like the original, dirty words to "The Star Spangled Banner", Lincoln's predilection for little boys, and the fact that the Pilgrims were actually huge sissies who spent most of their spare time crying over every little thing, like their impeding starvation and the fact that their hats only came in two colors: "black" and "fuck you, you'll take it in black". That's what makes Solomon Kane such an interesting cat - essentially, he's a pilgrim, but he's also a straight-up badass who travels the world fighting monsters and evil. (The latter generally being defined as anything he doesn't understand. Pilgrims are Christians, after all.) He was invented by the same guy who came up with Conan the Barbarian, Kull of Atlantis, and Red Sonja, and once Hollywood had trashed all three of those properties (the latter by casting Brigitte Nielsen – quite possibly the only chick on the planet who doesn't look hot dressed as Red Sonja – as Red Sonja, and Arnold Schwarzenegger as a barbarian who isn't Conan, but who looks and acts exactly like Conan, one assumes solely to fuck with us), they set their sights on Solomon Kane with typically shitty results. The story's your usual generic pap about an evil wizard and his marauding army of pricks wreaking endless havoc until finally one man stands up to them and, with a small band of loyal followers, raids their crib to save the fair-to-middlin' maiden. Solomon Kane is crucified, barely avoids being eaten by zombies, punks a witch, fights a demon, blah blah blah... It's all suitably dark and badass without being in any way original or engaging, and despite the fact that Solomon Kane is a pretty interesting and unique character this flick basically treats him like a less-buff Conan with a better wardrobe, and seems blissfully unaware that this story should be taking place in Pilgrim times (approximately 1600-1700 AD), not some vague, Middle Earth/Dungeons & Dragons era. It's a near-miss in the same way that the Ranger 3 space probe was a near-miss, and I'm glad that it's finally available in North America after a long delay because frankly I was pretty damn tired of hearing nerds whine about how awesome it *probably* was. Seriously, you fucking nerds will champion anything you can't actually get your hands on, won't you? *The Star Wars Holiday Special.*

Son of Sinbad

(1955)

Directed by Ted Tetzlaff

Your better Sinbad movies generally showcase a menagerie of cool mythological monsters, but I guess this one didn't have the budget for that so they do the next best thing and showcase a bevy of hot chicks instead. It all begins when Dr. Phibes catches his buddy Sinbad sneaking into a harem to score some ass. They're both quickly arrested, but then events conspire in such a way that they're offered a chance to win back their freedom if they help the king track down some Greek fire to use against the barbarians who want to invade the city. Sinbad and Phibes team up with a horde of sexy chicks, obtain the Greek fire, beat the barbarians' asses, and save the day. The end. The whole thing plays out like a nudie movie with no tits, but there are several impressive dancing girls, plus some hilarious sexism, like the part where this guy says that a girl with a brain "must be a rare creature indeed," or the scene where another cat elbows a plate of fruit right into some broad's face. If you've got a relatively low opinion of chicks, you might want to check this one out.

The Sword and the Sorcerer

(1982)

Directed by Albert Pyun

This flick is well-regarded as one of the few trashy sword and sorcery flicks that actually delivers, and most people who saw it back in the day fondly remember the demon tearing that chick's heart out and the main guy's absurd/awesome sword that sports three parallel blades (see, it's a *triple* sword), two of which can be launched like rockets to impale people from a distance. And those things are cool, but what everyone seems to forget is that the demon eats it like a bitch almost immediately and does practically nothing else until the very end of the film, and the main guy only uses his amazing Airsoft sword a grand total of twice. The rest of the movie is primarily political maneuverings and home invasions, most of which are, inexplicably, directed against the bad guy. (Truth be told, so many different individuals have it in for the bad guy that it's a wonder the good guy even makes it to the front of the line.) It's all violent enough, there are some tits, and they did recruit a pretty amazing all-hack cast (including Matt Houston, Buz Murdock, Manimal, Bull from *Night Court*, the 1970's Captain America, and Kirby from *Dynasty* as the chick everyone wants to fuck, including, apparently, the snake) so it isn't a *terrible* movie, but it definitely doesn't deserve its reputation as a ludicrous, over-the-top classic.

Incidentally, the sequel they promise at the end – *Tales of the Ancient Empire* – finally happened in 2010 as *Tales of AN Ancient Empire*, and no wonder it took so long with a generic tell-nothing title like that. Seriously, I wonder how many focus groups it took to make the monumental decision to change "the" to "an"? What a bunch of tools. If they were smart, they would've called it "Sword and the Sorcerer II: Blood and Tits".

Tall Tale

(1995)

Directed by Jeremiah S. Chechik

Well I'll be horngoggled if this ain't the gun-slingin'est, root-tootin'est, ass-suckin'est bag of shit I ever did see. Some crooks want this joker's land, and when he won't sell, they shoot him. His kid runs off with the deed though, and said kid's brilliant followup plan is to take a nap, during which he has a ridiculous dream wherein Paul Bunyan (© 1914 the Red River Lumber Company), Pecos Bill (© 1917 folklore) and... er, some other guy (Long John Silver?) teach him to stand up for what he believes in. When the kid wakes up he does just that, so the bad guys shoot him too. The end. Ha! I'm kidding, of course, but I wish that was how this pissbag movie had ended though because at least that would've been interesting. Normally when you hear about folklore guys they're doing unbelievable shit like punching a fool so hard that he lands on the moon, or cutting down a tree that's so tall it takes over a week for it to hit the ground, or eating so much pussy that they actually have to go on a diet afterwards. That's why their stories are called "tall tales" (or "bullshit"). In this movie though, pretty much all they do is shoot people and get into brawls. Hell, I could do that. Where, exactly, is the "tall tale" part? Screw this lousy ripoff. Fucking weak.

The Thief and the Cobbler

(1993)

Directed by Richard Williams

So, the legend (or "tall tale") goes that the jackass who created this cartoon started it in 1964 but didn't actually finish the goddamned thing until 1993 (that must have been one hell of a bender), and in the meantime Disney's *Aladdin* completely ripped him off. Well, there are a lot of similarities, but asking Disney not to steal is like asking a fish not to swim, so it's not like that should come as a big surprise to anyone. And frankly it seems like this movie ripped off just as much from Disney along the way, so fuck your hypocrite whining. For example, the bad guy's bird in *The Thief and the Cobbler* sounds just like the bad guy's bird in *Aladdin*, but his beak doesn't move when he talks and he never actually says anything pertinent to the plot, which leads me to believe that his voice was a total lift that they just dubbed in later. At any rate, the real problem with this flick, as it turns out, is the thief. Every single joke and pointless, obvious comment he makes is so fucking annoying and unfunny that I could barely stand it. Seriously, it took literally forever for me to watch this, because every time the thief said *anything* I was compelled to stop the tape and storm around the office for a while, ranting and raving about how fucking stupid it was. I was screaming about the thief for so long that the guy who runs the paki mart next door actually came over to ask if we'd been robbed and should he call the police. I told him only if they could track down Jonathan Winters, the voice of the thief in *The Thief and the Cobbler*, so I could personally kick his fat ass back to No Talentville, where he clearly keeps a summer house that also doubles as his rest-of-the-year house. Instead of sympathizing though, he said I was nuts and he'd rather I didn't patronize his store any more. Fucking dick. So not only did I waste half a day getting through this awful cartoon, but now I have to walk two extra blocks if I need to buy beer while I'm at work.

Thanks a lot, *Thief and the Cobber*, you miserable piece of shit. Fuck you.

Thor: Hammer of the Gods

(2009)

Directed by Todor Chapkanov

Remember that goofy idiot in the first Conan the Barbarian movie, the one with the hysterically big hammer? I was really hoping Thor would be more like that guy, all over-the-top and ridiculous, but no such luck. Instead, he looks like an out-of-shape grad student and sports a fauxhawk. The story is basically "Vikings vs. werewolves", which sounds cool in theory but keep in mind that this has been filtered through the Sci-Fi Channel, which has the same general effect as filtering a hamburger through your colon. To be fair this movie is less of a sack than most Sci-Fi Channel flicks, but it's still a sack; hell, I'm still not sure if the viking cats featured here are supposed to *be* the Norse gods, or if they all just happen to be *named after* the Norse gods. That would be quite the coincidence though, wouldn't it? It would be like if every single one of your friends was called "Allah". The only high point is the three-way chick fight between the main werewolf chick (who is fine beyond words) and two hot viking babes (er, *were* there girl vikings? Probably not, but right now who cares?), but it's not like they're in bikinis or anything so if all you're looking for is a flick to hammer *your* god to, I suggest you look elsewhere.

The Threat of the Odaku

(2005)

Produced for the Mega Bloks Dragons: Metal Ages toy line

This DVD came with a toy dragon I bought, and I really have to ask: does every single toy line have to come pre-loaded with some ludicrously complicated backstory? When I was a kid I made up my own stories, and all my toys interacted with each other regardless of scale or logic, which was too bad for some of them. When a 5½" He-Man figure rapes a 3¾" Princess Leia figure, that's gotta hurt.

So, it seems that the "Odaku" are huge dicks who raise evil dragons (that somehow hatch from their eggs already wearing armor) and use them to run roughshod over everybody. These other blowhards decide to stand up to the Odaku though, so an Odaku dragon makes off with one of the blowhards' leaders, which instigates a raid on the Ramparts of something-or-other, where the evil queen Skylla dwells, protected by the Lodestone Crystal. Fortunately, her Lieutenant, Gorhehar, sells her out to Dev and the Dragons of Light, so... so...

Arrrrrgggghhhh!!!!!

Are you fucking kidding me? I can't believe someone got paid good, cash money to come up with a *Silmarillion*-level epic for a bunch of goddamned Lego knockoffs to act out! Seriously, I would love to know how many fucking man-hours actually went into writing this garbage. What qualifies a person for a job like that anyway? "Yeah, I can make up a bunch of names that sound like they were plucked out of a Dungeons & Dragons module, and I have no shame." "You're hired." Jesus H. God, the world is completely retarded. Fuck this bullshit.

On the plus side, now that I've published a review of this moronic DVD it's officially a business expense, which means I can write off that toy dragon on my taxes. Sweet.

Universal's Islands of Adventure: Eighth Voyage of Sindbad

(Fall, 2010 Performance)

Universal Studios, Orlando, Florida

You can only watch so many Syphilis Channel movies before you're constantly seeing cartoon monsters out of the corner of your eye. This isn't scary or anything because naturally they look completely fake, but it is annoying so in the Fall of 2010 I decided to give the TV a break and review something a little different. And that's how I ended up at Universal's Islands of Overpriced Adventure with my two associates: a hot chick who wouldn't throw it out (rest assured, I'll deal with her later), and a guy who was hung over the entire time which needless to say was hilarious. Especially after we rode the roller coaster. But this entry isn't about someone throwing up all over "Toon Lagoon" or me furiously masturbating in my hotel room while vowing revenge. This entry is about the Sindbad stunt show, and how much it sucks.

First off, I guess I should give them props for spelling "Sindbad" right, even though nobody who speaks English actually spells it that way so I don't know who they're trying to impress except maybe the Muslims. You Homeland Security types might want to look into that. As for the show itself, well, the stunts are okay, and you might actually be impressed if you've never seen an action movie or someone fall off the roof before. The little adventure they play out is shitty beyond belief though. Basically, Sindbad and his annoying sidekick have to rescue a princess from this evil witch (both of these chicks were fucking hideous, by the way), which sounds passable enough and probably would've been if the whole thing wasn't full of awful, unfunny jokes and references to celebrities that I'm guessing they update with find/replace every, oh, ten years or so. (Then again, there was, I kid you not, a Mr. T gag, so it's probably closer to every thirty years.) And let's not forget that old standby, farting. Seriously, the asshole who wrote this show should be drowned in a river of his own piss. Now, I know what you're thinking: "It's all about the stunts, Mr. Satanism, not the story. Lighten up." Fuck that. Why can't both be good? For real, playing right across from this I.Q.-ravaging disaster was another show called *Poseidon's Fury*, where you stroll through a building while special effects ejaculate all around you. There was only one actor and he had to carry the entire thing, but he did an awesome job and it was actually pretty cool. Take my advice: visit that one twice and forget the *Eighth Voyage of Sindbad*. It's a wretched, garment-rending pile of camel dung.

Warrior Queen

(1987)

Directed by Chuck Vincent

Our story takes place in Pompeii, which is primarily known for exploding. What are the odds that this will play into the narrative somehow? The titular (heh) warrior queen is Sybil Danning, best known for being overrated, not that this matters since her appearance here barely amounts to an extended cameo. Seriously, I wish I would've counted the actual number of words she says during the entirety of this movie. I'll bet it's less than twenty. Anyway, while in Pompeii on business she's treated to a sampling of degenerate Roman antics, like people arm wrestling to the death (take that, *Over the Top*), warriors engaged in gimmicky duels that aren't gimmicky enough to actually be interesting, and the inevitable parade of second-rate nudity, treachery, vanilla dyking out, and crowd shots lifted from another movie. She looks bored, I was bored, and you'll be bored, unless you've never seen tits before, and the Internet exists so obviously you have. To be fair, there is a little gore, and some half-hearted rape, but in a world where *Caligula* (1979) exists this flick doesn't go anywhere near far enough. In the end, the best part is probably this exchange:

SCORNED CHICK: "You loved me once."

RAKE: "I've loved many women once."

Ha ha! It is ancient Rome, so he's probably blowing her off so he can go fuck some teenage boys or something, but that's still pretty funny.

The Witch's Curse

(1962)

Directed by Riccardo Freda

This cat burns some old bag at the stake because she wouldn't give him any play when she was younger, and 100 years later the curse the old bag subsequently laid down is still causing everyone grief. So when this babe with the same name arrives in town, the villagers decide they'd better burn her at the stake too. Because that worked so well before. Fortunately, a muscleman from a completely different genre picks this exact moment to ride into town to buy some pants, and he's just in time to rescue her. Afterward the chick decides to file a grievance with the mayor, but the needs of the many registered voters outweigh the needs of the one so he predictably sides with the villagers. (Of course, it probably doesn't help the chick's cause that when she tries to swear on the Bible the Ventures' "Wipeout" kicks in and the entire book bursts into flames.) The muscleman decides to go to Hell to straighten this shit out, where he gets attacked by a lion (the fake lion head they use in this part looked naggingly familiar, and trust me, if you watch enough of these paplum movies you really do start to recognize specific prop lion heads); gets sidetracked by pussy ("How is it that a beautiful woman like you is down here?" he says, because, as we all know, beautiful people only go to Heaven); fights a giant; strangles an eagle; has a long, time-killing flashback to previous muscleman flicks he's starred in; completely owns a stampede; and finally brings an end to the curse by kissing the witch in front of her would-be boyfriend, who proceeds to furiously flail his arms around and then fall down a hill in a comical fashion.

I'll tell ya, I really cannot get enough of this shit.

Wizards of the Demon Sword

(1991)

Directed by Fred Olen Ray

How does one come up with a title like "Wizards of the Demon Sword"? Do you cut up a page from an old Conan novel and then draw pieces of it out of a hat? However they came up with it, *The Sword of Demon Wizards* opens with some dudes chasing a mediocre piece of ass through the desert. And when I say "mediocre", trust me when I tell you that I'm being generous. Eventually they catch her, but then who should appear but a buff queer sporting a sword so big that [insert your own penis joke here]. He saves the distressed damsel, and then agrees to help rescue her dad (played by Laura Palmer's doctor, who, it appears, is a shitty actor in everything) from the bad guys. Along the way they see (but don't interact with) several dinosaurs lifted from the infinitely better movie *Planet of Dinosaurs* (1977), confer with the "Seer of Roebuck" (I assume this is supposed to be comedy), fight with some desert folk (you know, like your uncle's always doing), and accidentally wander into the original *Hills Have Eyes* for a scene. Several bad jokes leave one with the impression that this is trying to be a "funny" sword & sorcery movie, but

Deathstalker II remains the gold standard in that category and rest assured that *The Demon Sword of Wizards* is no *Deathstalker II*. It's not funny, it's not exciting, and the only member of the cast who does a decent job is the actress playing the evil chick, who dies quite convincingly at the end and, furthermore, quite convincingly made me want to fuck her, despite the fact that she really wasn't all that hot. See, ladies, looks are important, but having the right attitude matters at least as much. Dressing like a cross between Wendy O. Williams and Thundarr's whore sister doesn't hurt either.

Wrath of the Titans (Graphic Novel)

(2008)

Written by Darren G. Davis and Scott Davis

With the possible exception of this sorority chick I dated in the 1980's ("Ohmigod it would be so radical to have a flying horse! I want a flying horse!") I can't think of anyone who was waiting for *Clash of the Titans Part 2*, but in 2008 it turned up anyway, in comic book form, which is the latest place pointless sequels and TV shows no one cares about anymore go when they refuse to die. Unfortunately, even if you think this is the greatest thing to happen since you scored that original Kraken figure, mint-in-package, off eBay, this comic is so rambling and nonsensical that I dare you to figure out what the hell is supposed to be happening in it. Of course, most of the old movies the original *Clash of the Titans* guy worked on tended to ramble too, but they still managed to rock because they were stuffed to the gills with his cool-ass monsters. And this brings us to the other major problem with this comic: it is full of monsters, but all they did was recycle the ones from the movies! There's the flying horse and the robot owl from *Clash of the Titans*, which does make some narrative sense, but they also break out the seven-headed dragon from *Jason and the Argonauts*, the cyclops from *Seventh Voyage of Sinbad*, and even the saber-toothed tiger from *Sinbad and the Eye of the Walrus*! Are you fucking kidding me??? For real, they couldn't be bothered to dream up *any* new monsters? If this were a movie sequel I could fully understand recycling the monster models that were already built, but it's a fucking *comic book!* You can *draw* anything! Well, you can if you have any talent or imagination, anyway. Seriously, I cannot believe how lazy and unimaginative this is. Four years later they actually did make a *Wrath of the Titans* movie, but it had nothing to do with the original *Clash of the Titans* or this comic, and by all accounts it was an even bigger piece of shit than this version is. Seeing that the movie is undoubtedly an orgy of cartoon effects and the computers that made it also could've "drawn" anything, it's pretty pathetic that they couldn't come up with a decent take on this concept either. What a bunch of fucking hacks. Give me Sinbad fighting that gigantic walrus any day.

Don't miss out!

Visit the website below and you can sign up to receive emails whenever Mr. Satanism publishes a new book. There's no charge and no obligation.

https://books2read.com/r/B-A-TCXC-HBLJ

BOOKS2READ

Connecting independent readers to independent writers.

Also by Mr. Satanism

66.6 Absurd Movies About the Devil
Legendary House of Haunted Hell
Trash of the Titans
Night of the Living Dud
Lifetime Movies... for Men
Shark Weak: The Worst Shark Movies Ever Made
The Not-At-All-Cleverly-Titled Book of Dragon Movies
Snakes, Rats, Spiders, and Bats: A Creepy-Crawly Movie
Compendium
Monkeys & Dinosaurs: Cinema as High Art, Vol. 1
Hex Crimes: The Worst Witch Movies Ever Made
Close Encounters of the Worst Kind
Triskaidekaphilia - Mr. Satanism's 13th Book
Vampire Movies Suck
Werewolves Don't Eat Brunch
Mr. Satanism's Invisible Book
A Yeti Brew (And Bigfoot Too)
The Magical Golden Rainbow Book of Crappy Wizard of Oz
Movies
Cannibal Attraction
A Chronology on Elm Street
Mr. Satanism Puts Down Your Favorite Dog (...Movies)
A Collection of Woke Movie Reviews